D1250386

THE DESPERATE HOURS

THE

A play by

**JOSEPH
HAYES**

*Based on
the novel
by the same
author*

*Random House
New York*

DESPERATE HOURS

For Marrijane

THE DESPERATE HOURS was first presented by Howard Erskine and Joseph Hayes at the Ethel Barrymore Theatre, New York City, on February 10, 1955, with the following cast:

(IN ORDER OF APPEARANCE)

TOM WINSTON	Judson Pratt
JESSE BARD	James Gregory
HARRY CARSON	Kendall Clark
ELEANOR HILLIARD	Nancy Coleman
RALPHIE HILLIARD	Malcolm Brodrick
DAN HILLIARD	Karl Malden
CINDY HILLIARD	Patricia Peardon
GLENN GRIFFIN	Paul Newman
HANK GRIFFIN	George Grizzard
ROBISH	George Mathews
CHUCK WRIGHT	Fred Eisley
MR. PATTERSON	Wyrley Birch
LT. CARL FREDERICKS	Rusty Lane
MISS SWIFT	Mary Orr

Setting and lighting by Howard Bay

Staged by Robert Montgomery

Costumes by Robert Randolph

Time: The present.

Scene: The City of Indianapolis.

ACT ONE
A day in autumn

ACT TWO
Later

ACT THREE
Later

SCENE

The action throughout the play alternates between two sets on stage. In the first two acts, the Hilliard home is at stage-right and the Sheriff's office is at stage-left. In ACT THREE, *the Hilliard home is at stage-right, and at stage-left is a corner of an attic room. The action shifts back and forth between the two sets by the use of blackouts and sliding black curtains which mask the set that is not in focus.*

The Hilliard home is the principal set. This consists of various rooms, all blended together by fluid action; lights focus the attention in the various rooms, as the action of the play requires.

On the ground-floor level of the house, there are two rooms in view at all times: the living room and a back hall or pantry. In the living room, there is an outside door in the rear wall; next to this door are stairs rising to the upstairs level. At right a door gives access to a den or library, off-stage. At left, facing downstage, there is another door; this door, presumably, leads into a dining room; the dining room is adjacent to a kitchen; the kitchen door opens into the pantry or back hall. In this manner, a character leaving the living room exits through the dining-room door and in a moment reappears in the pantry. This pantry is a small room in itself. In addition to the kitchen door, there is an exterior side door of the house itself opening off the pantry at stage-left. Back stairs descend along the exterior wall at left: a narrow passageway gives access to the upper floor. The entire ground floor, then, consists of a living room with front stairs curving up, a front door, a door to the den and a door to the dining room; a pantry with a door to the kitchen, an exterior side door, shelves, and a narrow stairway going up. In addition, a portion of the side yard is visible at left.

The upper level—constructed above the ground-floor level described above—consists of two bedrooms and an upstairs hall between; this hall gives access to the downward flow of the front stairway. The bedroom at stage-right is the master bedroom, containing twin beds, windows right and up-center, and a bureau. The bedroom at stage-left is a boy's bedroom, with a bunk, various shelves with toys, and a window overlooking the side yard. Between the two bedrooms is a small hall: downstage is a small table with a telephone.

At far left stage, during the first two acts, is the Sheriff's office on ground level, a bare sort of room with a wall-clock, a desk, various files, and radio and intercom apparatus. In the last act, a corner of an attic appears at stage-left; this is constructed above the Sheriff's office, and in ACT THREE *the office is completely masked.*

ACT ONE

ACT ONE

SHERIFF'S OFFICE

The curtain rises, morning light fades in on the Sheriff's office. WINSTON, *a deputy sheriff inclined to matter-of-fact laziness, sits at desk, speaking on the telephone. On the desk are an intercom, radio apparatus, sheafs of papers, and so forth. The wall-clock reads 8:10.*

WINSTON
(Plaintively)

Baby . . . didn't I just tell you? I can't leave till Bard gets here. (*He listens*) Listen, baby—this night shift gets my goat as much as it does yours. You think I wouldn't like to be in that nice warm bed? (*There is a buzz from the intercom on the desk*) Hold it. (*He speaks into the intercom*) Yeah, Dutch?

DUTCH'S VOICE

Winston . . . Bard's going to want those Terre Haute reports right away.

WINSTON
(Irascibly, into intercom)

What do you think I'm gonna do with 'em . . . eat 'em for breakfast? (*He flips off the intercom, returns to the phone*) Hello, baby . . . (*Listens*) Yeah, that's what I said, isn't it? In that nice warm bed *with you.* Who'd you think I . . . (*Listens*) Okay, okay, baby . . . go back to sleep and wait for Papa. (*Hangs up, shakes head, pleased; speaks with gusto*) Give me a jealous woman every time!

> (BARD *enters.* WINSTON *is sleepy and glad to be relieved.* BARD *takes off jacket, removes gun from shoulder-holster through the following. All very casual and commonplace at first.*)

3

BARD

(As he enters)

Morning, Tom.

WINSTON

(Stretching)

Well! About time.

BARD

(Stows gun in drawer of file)

Overslept. Sorry.

WINSTON

(Rising slowly)

You got a lovely excuse.

BARD

I'll tell her you think so. *(Above desk, riffles reports)* Quiet night?

WINSTON

(Preparing to go)

If kids'd stay out of cars and off motorcycles, we'd soon be out of jobs around here.

BARD

Not another burglary in Speedway City? *(Laughs)* This guy's getting tiresome.

WINSTON

A real sex-nut, that one. Same old story . . . all he took was diamonds and women's panties. What the hell's the connection.

BARD

You figure it out, Tom. *(Then tensing . . . so that from now on the pace and tone change)* What's this?

4

WINSTON

(*Yawns, looking over* BARD's *shoulder*)
Federal prison break ... Terre Haute. None of our concern.

BARD

When'd it come in?

WINSTON

(*Ready to leave*)
Hours ago. The three of 'em busted out some time before dawn. . . .

BARD

(*Sits at desk, snaps button on intercom*)
Why didn't you call me?

WINSTON

Call you? Why?

DUTCH'S VOICE

Yes, Jesse?

BARD

(*Into intercom*)
Dutch . . . get me Lieutenant Fredericks, State Police.

WINSTON

Jesse . . . remember what your Irish wife threatened last time I routed you out of the nest. . . .

BARD

Terre Haute's only seventy miles away. They could've *walked* here by now!

FREDERICKS' VOICE

(*On intercom—crisp, middle-aged, cynical*)
I wondered when you'd start yipping, Bard.

5

BARD
(*Quickly*)
Fredericks . . . anybody sitting on anything?

FREDERICKS' VOICE
I'm sitting on just what you're sitting on, Deputy. Only mine ain't sweatin'.

BARD
Griffin's woman . . . Helen Laski . . . any dope on her?

FREDERICKS' VOICE
Not a trace. Chicago . . . Cleveland . . . St. Louie. All we know is she was here in town three weeks ago.

BARD
Just don't let any cop touch her. She's the beacon'll lead us straight . . .

FREDERICKS' VOICE
Bard . . . it's an FBI case anyway. The city police've ripped whole buildings apart. We got the highways blocked. We're working through all the dives. . . .

BARD
If Glenn Griffin wants to come here, no roadblock's gonna stop him. And he's too sharp to hole up any place you'd think of looking.

FREDERICKS' VOICE
Look, lad . . . get that chip off your shoulder. (*Shortly*) You want Griffin so bad, go get him!
(BARD *flips off the intercom.* WINSTON *reluctantly removes his coat.*)

WINSTON
Glenn Griffin . . . is he the one you . . . ?

6

BARD

(*Thoughtfully*)

Yeah . . . he's the one. (*Studying reports*) Glenn Griffin . . . his brother, Hank . . . and . . . who's this third one? Samuel Robish.

WINSTON

Life-termer. A three-time loser. And nasty. (*As* BARD *picks up the phone and dials,* WINSTON *returns his coat to the hanger*) You're not going to get any sleep today, are you, Winston? No, I'm not going to get any sleep today. I'm going to sit on the teletype machine like a good little boy scout. . . .

> (BARD *smiles a bit as* WINSTON *exits. Then he speaks into the telephone in contrasting gentle tones.*)

BARD

Hello, Katie. Did I wake you? . . . I've just had an idea . . . why don't you go over to my mother's for the day? (*Laughs —but the urgency comes through*) Oh, stop groaning . . . how often do I ask you to *let* her talk your arm and leg off? . . . No, not this afternoon. *Now!* . . . And Katie . . . don't mention where you're going, huh? . . . To the neighbors, anyone . . . Good. . . . Right away. Take a taxi. . . . Sure, splurge.

> (BARD *hangs up, sits thinking, with the smile fading.* WINSTON *enters, with* CARSON, *who is youthful, businesslike, rather studious-looking.* WINSTON *places a teletype message on desk before* BARD.)

WINSTON

It had to break, Jesse. (*Then with a touch of sarcasm as* BARD *reads*) Oh—this is Mr. Carson, FBI.

BARD

(*Briskly*)

How are you? Look, it says they beat up a farmer south of the prison before daybreak. How come we're just getting it?

7

CARSON

They left him in his barn, out cold ... ripped out his phone. He just staggered into a general store and reported his car stolen. . . . (*With a touch of good-natured irony*) How are *you?*

BARD

Have you put this on the air?

CARSON

Deputy, I've been in touch with Sheriff Masters by telephone.

BARD

I hope he's enjoying his extended vacation ... he sure picked a fine time to leave me in charge here. . . .

CARSON

The way I understand it, you know this Glenn Griffin fellow better than any police officer in the area. How about your taking over this section?
(*Pause. The whole weight falls on* BARD. *He accepts it . . . slowly. Then:*)

BARD

Okay ... *Okay* ... Let's find that car! (*He goes into action —hands teletype to* WINSTON) Tom, put this description on the air. Tell 'em to repeat it every half hour.

WINSTON
(*Protesting*)
We'll be flooded with calls. Every crackpot in five states ...

BARD
(*Sitting at desk*)
We'll follow up every tip!

8

WINSTON
(*To* CARSON—*groaning*)
I hope you know what you just did!
(WINSTON *exits.* CARSON *moves to desk and offers* BARD
a cigarette.)

CARSON
Any ideas where they might dig in?

BARD
(*Shaking his head*)
All I know is . . . just as long's Glenn Griffin's running
around free and safe—with that prison guard's .38 in his paw
—well, it's not free or safe for anyone else. No decent people
anywhere—whether they've ever . . . (*The lights begin to
dim*) heard of Glenn Griffin or not . . .

HILLIARD HOME
*Lights rise slowly. We see the complete outline of
a typical house in the suburbs: pleasant, comfortable,
undistinguished.* ELEANOR HILLIARD, *an attractive
woman in her early forties, enters from the dining
room, moves to front door, opens it and looks out. The
morning light outside is bright and cheerful. Not find-
ing the morning paper, she closes the door as* RALPHIE
enters from dining room. RALPHIE, *aged ten, is dressed
for school and carries a half-empty glass of milk,
which he stares at balefully as he sits.* ELEANOR, *who
is extremely neat, is arranging pillows on the sofa.*

ELEANOR
(*Gently*)
Ralphie, you left your bike outside all night again.

RALPHIE
(*As though this answers her*)
It didn't rain.

9

ELEANOR

Well, it's not going to rain today, either. But you're going to put it in the garage before you go to school.

(DAN HILLIARD *enters from dining room and crosses to front door to look out. He is a typical, undistinguished but immediately likable man in his forties.*)

DAN

(*Calling up the stairs as he passes*)
Cindy! It's eight-thirty.

CINDY

(*Off, in her room upstairs*)
Can't a girl straighten her girdle in peace?

DAN

(*Surprised*)
Girdle? . . . Girdle! (*Goes to* ELEANOR) Ellie, can a twenty-year-old child with a figure like Cindy's . . .

ELEANOR

(*Smiling*)
It's a joke, Dan.

DAN

Oh. Thank the Lord. She has to have a solid hour for primping and then she complains all the way downtown because we don't live in the city limits.

RALPHIE

Ain't love disgusting?

ELEANOR

Don't say "ain't."

10

DAN

(*To* RALPHIE—*firmly*)

Don't say "love," either. (*There is a thud of a newspaper thrown against the front door.* DAN *steps swiftly to the door. He and* ELEANOR *have a slight collision. She moves downstage and he opens the door and goes off onto the porch*) Hey! *Hey!*

ELEANOR

(*Teasing*)

Try holding your nose and gulping it, Ralphie.

RALPHIE

It tastes sour.

ELEANOR

(*Picking up her small pad and pencil from coffee table*)

Yesterday it tasted like chalk.

　　　(*She sits and starts making her shopping list.* DAN *returns, picks up the* Indianapolis Star, *and enters the room, closing the door.*)

DAN

(*A suggestion of grouchiness*)

Some day I'm going to catch up with that paper boy and we're going to have a lawsuit on our hands.

ELEANOR

Dan, you have time for a second cup of coffee.

DAN

(*Glances at his watch and then up the stairs*)

In half a minute she'll come prancing down those stairs and start urging *me* to hurry.

　　　(DAN *exits into the dining room.* RALPHIE *takes a long drink of the milk but cannot finish it.* CINDY *comes down the stairs in time to see him.*)

11

CINDY

Well, *today* you are a man!
(*She goes to the closet, gets her coat and bag.*)

RALPHIE

If cows only knew how I hated 'em!

ELEANOR

What would they do?

CINDY

(*To* ELEANOR)
Where's Dad? What was he shouting at me?

ELEANOR

What does he shout every morning at eight-thirty?

CINDY

He shouts it's eight-thirty.

ELEANOR

You win the kewpie-doll.
(CINDY *moves swiftly toward the dining room as* DAN
appears in the door with a cup of coffee.)

CINDY

(*To* DAN *as she swings past him*)
Say, you'd better hurry!

DAN

(*Looks after* CINDY, *then to* ELEANOR *as he sits on sofa*)
What'd I tell you?
(DAN *sets his cup of coffee on the table and picks up
the newspaper and reads.*)

12

RALPHIE

Dad ... Why did the moron lock his father in the refrigerator?

DAN

(*His attention on the newspaper*)
Ralphie, do I have to answer that one?

RALPHIE

(*Brightly*)
Because he liked cold pop! (*There is an escape of breath from* DAN *which might or might not pass for a laugh*) Well, why don't you laugh?

DAN

I laughed. What do you want me to do . . . roll on the floor?

RALPHIE

You *almost* rolled on the floor last night when I told you why the moron ate dynamite.

ELEANOR

(*Shakes her head warningly but continues writing*)
Ralphie . . .

RALPHIE

My name is Ralph. R-a-l-p-h. There's no Y on the end of it. I looked up my birth certificate.

ELEANOR

Sorry.
(*Through the following,* RALPHIE *rises and, with glass in hand, moves to the chair by front door to pick up his jacket and football; he rather elaborately manages to conceal the half-glass of milk on the floor out of sight in the process.*)

13

RALPHIE

Big game after school today. Fourth grade versus fifth grade. (*Having achieved his purpose; with a sigh of relief*) We'll slaughter 'em!

(*Kisses* ELEANOR.)

ELEANOR

'Bye, darling.

(DAN *leans back to be kissed, but* RALPHIE *brushes past him and goes to dining-room door, where* DAN's *voice stops him.*)

DAN

Hey! Aren't you forgetting something?

RALPHIE

(*Embarrassed and uncertain*)

Oh. (*He then returns to* DAN, *who leans for a kiss; instead,* RALPHIE *extends his hand and shakes* DAN's *hand with grave formality*) So long, Dad. I hope you have a very pleasant day at the office. (*He turns and goes into the dining room, leaving* DAN *staring after him, then reappears in the pantry on his way to the side door*) So long, dream-witch. I hope Chuck Wright doesn't even notice your new dress.

CINDY

(*Steps into pantry with glass of orange juice in her hand*) 'Bye. Flunk geography, will you, pest?

RALPHIE

(*As he goes out the side door*)

Mister Pest to you.

ELEANOR

(*Calling from living room*)

Ralphie! Your bicycle!

14

DAN

What do you suppose that was all about?

ELEANOR

(*Toying with her pad and pencil*)

Our son Ralph . . . spelled R-a-l-p-h . . . considers himself too old to kiss a man . . . that's you . . . good-bye or good-night.

DAN

(*Covering his hurt*)

Oh.

ELEANOR

He said last night he hoped you'd understand.

DAN

(*With an empty smile*)

I was hoping maybe he just didn't like my shave-lotion. (*As* ELEANOR *unconsciously touches his hair*) Ellie, what's happening to both of them lately? This . . . this young lawyer Cindy works for . . . she can't be *serious,* can she?

ELEANOR

(*Sits*)

She hasn't confided in me, Dan . . . which could mean she is.

DAN

She's only twenty years old!

ELEANOR

I was nineteen.

DAN

You had some sense.

ELEANOR

Sure. I married you.

DAN

(*As though he has proved a point*)
Well, I didn't drive a Jaguar!
(CINDY *enters from the dining room and goes to put on her coat.*)

CINDY

Chuck and I find his Jaguar a very comfortable little sur-rey. Come climb into my Ford coupé, Dad . . . and don't whisper when I'm in the next room. It's not polite.

DAN

(*As he rises and moves to closet*)
Now she'll speed.

ELEANOR

(*Automatically*)
Careful now, Dan.

CINDY

(*Satirically—chidingly*)
Mother . . . you say that every morning of the world. What could possibly happen to a man in the personnel of-fice of a department store?
(*She exits, closing the door.*)

DAN

(*Pointing at closed door*)
That's what I mean! That's not Cindy. Those are Chuck Wright's ideas. Last night on the way home, she asked me point-blank if I didn't think I led a pretty dull life.

ELEANOR

What'd you say?

16

DAN

(*Firmly*)

I said I didn't like Chuck Wright, either.

(DAN *goes to the door, and* ELEANOR *follows him.*)

ELEANOR

Dan . . . at Chuck's age . . . you were going to be another Richard Halliburton, remember? Climb the Matterhorn . . . swim at midnight in the Taj Mahal. My father threatened to throw you . . .

(*Outside,* CINDY *taps horn impatiently.*)

DAN

I'm going to be late. (*They kiss: casual, without meaning, habit*) If you're going to use the car today, buy some gas first. *Before* you have to walk a mile for it this time.

(DAN *exits.* ELEANOR *closes the door.* ELEANOR *leans against the door a second, utters an almost silent "Whew," puts her shopping list and pencil on the telephone table, pushes her hair back from her forehead, pushes up her sleeves and prepares to begin the day. She moves to sofa, folds the newspaper and straightens the cushions. Then she goes upstairs, casually humming, and into* RALPHIE's *room. She shakes her head and begins to gather up the soiled clothes. She flips on a small portable radio and takes the clothes down the hall, presumably to the bathroom, disappears.*)

NEWSCASTER'S VOICE

. . . five-state alarm. Police authorities have requested all citizens to be on the lookout for a 1941 Dodge sedan . . . gray . . . mud-spattered . . . bearing Indiana license plates number HL6827 . . . that is HL6827. . . . One of the convicts is wearing a pair of faded blue farmer's overalls which were . . .

(ELEANOR *has returned and flips the radio to music.*
The music plays through the scene. ELEANOR *starts to*
make RALPHIE's *bed. The door chimes sound.*)

ELEANOR

Wouldn't you know it . . . every time . . . (*The chimes*
sound again, insistently. She comes down the stairs, but be-
fore she reaches the last step the chimes are heard for the
third time. She crosses to the door and opens it) Yes? (*The*
young man who stands there . . . still out of sight . . . is in
his mid-twenties and wears faded blue farmer's overalls. He
is tall with—at the moment—a rather appealing boyish ex-
pression on his handsome face.)

GLENN

Sorry to bother you, ma'am, but it looks like I lost my way.
(*As he speaks,* ROBISH *and* HANK GRIFFIN *appear outside and*
enter the house by the side door, stealthily) Could you kindly
direct me to the Bowden Dairy? I know it's somewhere in
the neighborhood, but I must have the wrong . . .

(HANK GRIFFIN—*who is younger than* GLENN, *shorter,*
not so handsome, with a confused, hard but somehow
rather sensitive face—remains in the pantry, looking
out the window of the side door. ROBISH *is large, bull-*
like, slow, with a huge head sunk between two bulky
upthrust shoulders. He goes into the kitchen at once
and reappears in the dining-room door. Both wear
prison garb. The following action has a cold, machine-
like precision about it.)

ELEANOR

(*Her back to the room*)
Let me see. I've seen that sign. But there are no dairies
very close. You see, this is a residential . . .

(ROBISH *now stands in the room.* ELEANOR *becomes*
conscious of his presence. She breaks off and turns.

In that moment GLENN *whips out the gun, forces his way into the room, pushing* ELEANOR. *He slams the door and locks it, then moves down to* ELEANOR.)

GLENN

Take it easy, lady. (*As her mouth trembles open*) Easy, I said. You scream, the kid owns that bike out there'll come home an' find you in a pool of blood. (GLENN *only nods to* ROBISH, *who stumps up the stairs and through the following looks into* CINDY'S *room,* RALPHIE'S *room, then enters the master bedroom and searches*) You there, Hank?

HANK

(*Speaking as he moves into the living room*)
All clear out back. Lincoln in garage . . . almost new. Garage lock broken.
(ELEANOR *looks at* HANK, *who returns her stare boldly. A shudder goes through her. Through the following,* GLENN'S *swagger suggests a deep insecurity. Above,* ROBISH *is examining and discarding various of* DAN'S *clothes in the bedroom . . . creating havoc.* GLENN *steps to* ELEANOR.)

GLENN

I'll take the keys to the Lincoln now, lady . . .

ELEANOR

Keys? . . . (*Conquering shudders*) Keys? . . .

GLENN

Lady, when I talk, you snap. Snap fast!

ELEANOR

Top of . . . top of refrigerator . . . I think . . . I always misplace the . . . (*As* GLENN *nods to* HANK, *who goes*

19

into dining room then into pantry with the keys and out the side door and off) Take it .. you only want the car . . . take it and go. . . .

GLENN

(*Shouts toward the stairs*)
What're you doin' up there, Robish—takin' a bath?

ROBISH

Nobody home but the missus.
(*He goes into upstairs hall, with* DAN's *clothes.*)

GLENN

I figured it. (*He examines the house . . . looks into the den*) Good-lookin' family you got, lady. I seen 'em leavin'. (*As* ROBISH *descends*) How many bedrooms up there, Robish?

ROBISH

Four. An' two complete cans, for Chrissake. . . .
(*The sound of a car door being slammed startles* ELEANOR.)

GLENN

Don't be so jumpy, lady. Only the kid brother takin' care of the cars.

ROBISH

(*Holding up* DAN's *suit*)
Th' sonofabitch's got five suits up there.
(*He tosses the suit over the back of chair and goes into the dining room . . . to reappear a few moments later searching the shelves in the pantry.*)

GLENN

Class, all the way. . . . (*To* ELEANOR) I guess you're tumbling to the idea, ain't you, lady?

20

ELEANOR
(Picks up her purse from sofa)
You want money . . . here . . . take it . . . anything . . .

GLENN
(Takes purse and dumps contents on sofa)
Pretty. *(Holds up a locket)* Gold? *(As* ELEANOR *nods wordlessly, he slips it into his pocket)* I got a gal with a yen for gold a mile wide. *(Picks up the money)* This all the dough you got in the house?

ELEANOR
(With difficulty)
Yes . . . yes . . . my husband always says . . . too much cash in . . .

GLENN
(Grins)
Old man's right. Ain't ever safe to have too much cash layin' around. *(He pockets the money)* Gives people ideas.
*(*ROBISH *returns, disgruntled.)*

ROBISH
(To GLENN*)*
My gut's growlin'.

GLENN
We heard it.

ROBISH
(To ELEANOR*)*
Missus, where you keep th' liquor?

ELEANOR
(Backing away from him to chair, sits)
We don't have . . . I don't think we . . .
*(*HANK *enters the side door, locks it.)*

GLENN

(*Gesturing to den*)

Robish . . . park your butt'n there'n keep your eyes peeled that side-a th' house.

ROBISH

(*Aggressively; to* ELEANOR)

I ain't had me a drink'n eighteen years.

GLENN

Robish, you don't hear so good. It's a kinda library. Improve your mind.

(HANK *enters from dining room.*)

HANK

Gray job's in the garage, outta sight. Lincoln's ready in the driveway . . . headin' out. But she's low on gas.

(*He hands the car keys to* GLENN, *who pockets them.*)

ROBISH

(*Stolidly*)

I need me a gun. (GLENN *nods to* HANK, *who turns and runs upstairs. Through the following, he looks into* CINDY's *room,* RALPHIE's *room, and enters the master bedroom, where he searches through the top bureau drawer, tossing out handkerchiefs and other odds and ends of clothing*) I don't like none of it.

GLENN

(*Calling up the stairs*)

Hey, Hank, Robish don't like it. After them hard bunks . . . them concrete floors!

HANK

Tell 'im to lump it.

GLENN

Lump it. Robish. (*Gestures to den*) In there.

ROBISH

I don't feel right without a gun.

GLENN

Tell you what, Robish . . . Let's you'n me go out an' stick up a hardware store!

ROBISH

Now you're talkin'!

GLENN

(*Sardonically*)

Sure . . . Come'n, Robish. Every copper'n the state's waitin' for us to pull a job like that! (*Moves to door*) What're you stallin' for? (HANK *finds an automatic in the drawer and pockets it and starts back downstairs*) Come on!

ROBISH

(*Turning away—growling, inwardly seething*)

Awwww . . . don't do me no favors. (*For the first time,* GLENN *laughs.* HANK, *watching* ROBISH, *joins in.* ELEANOR *stares.* ROBISH's *face hardens and, scowling, he makes a sudden movement toward* HANK) What're yuh yakkin' at, yuh . . .

(*But* GLENN *moves. The laughter dies. He grabs* ROBISH, *whips him about.*)

GLENN

(*In low hard tones*)

Lissen! How many times I gotta tell you? Keep your mitts off the kid, you don't wanna get your skull laid open. (*Pause.* ROBISH *and* GLENN *face each other. Then* ROBISH *turns sullenly and grabs suit of clothes, growling.* GLENN, *having as-*

23

serted his total control, laughs, takes cigar from humidor on coffee table and tosses it to ROBISH) Here . . . make yourself sick on a good cigar.

> (ROBISH, *seething, doesn't attempt to catch it; it falls to the floor. Then, defiantly,* ROBISH *steps on it, grinding it into the carpet.*)

GLENN

Robish, you gonna give the lady the idea we ain't neat.

ROBISH
(*He picks up the humidor*)
Coupla brothers! Shoulda knowed better. Ain't neither one dry back-a the ears yet.
> (ROBISH *exits into the den.*)

ELEANOR
(*Who has been watching in horror*)
What . . . what do you . . . ?

GLENN
(*Ignoring her, crosses to* HANK)
What'd you find? (HANK, *keeping his eyes on* ELEANOR, *takes the automatic out of his pocket and hands it to* GLENN, *who examines it.* GLENN, *to* ELEANOR) Lady, now I ask you . . . is that a nice thing to keep aroun' the house? (*He hands the automatic to* HANK, *whispering*) Put it in your pocket and keep it there. Family secret, huh? What Robish don't know, don't hurt nobody . . . okay? (GLENN *laughs, gives* HANK *a playful push and goes to chair in high spirits*) Let 'em comb the dives!

HANK
(*Sits on sofa; jubilantly*)
You foxed 'em good, Glenn.

GLENN

Came aroun' their roadblocks like we was flyin' a air-plane! Everything's chimin'! (*He sits in the armchair, be-comes conscious of the comfort. He raises himself by the arms and sinks again into the chair, delighted*) Foam rub-ber, I betcha. Foam rubber, lady? (ELEANOR *nods*) I seen the ads. (*He squirms in the seat, enjoying it*) Melts right into your tail!

HANK

(*Takes a cigarette from the box on the coffee table, lights it with the table lighter and, rising, hands it to* GLENN)
Christ, what a place to take the stir-taste outta your mouth! Freezer full-a meat! Carpet makes you want to take your shoes off!

ELEANOR

How long do you intend to . . .

GLENN

(*Casually*)
Be outta here by midnight, lady.

HANK

Midnight? I thought you said Helen was waiting . . .

GLENN

Not in town, Hank. We don't make it so easy for 'em. She left three weeks ago.

HANK

(*Laughs, rises, grabs a fistful of cigarettes from the box on the coffee table, picks up the lighter, and flips it several times in her face*)
I don't care if we never leave.
(*He exits into the dining room and reappears in the pantry, where he stands looking out the window of the side door.*)

25

GLENN

(*Rises*)

Now, lady . . . you think you can talk on the phone without bustin' into tears?

ELEANOR

(*Rises with great difficulty, takes a feeble step, then gets control of herself, straightens, and walks with dignity and determination to the phone table, turns to face* GLENN)

Whom do you want me to call?

(GLENN *laughs.*)

GLENN

I always go for a gal with guts! That's *whom* we're gonna call—a gal with real guts. Person to person . . . Mr. James calling Mrs. James . . . Atlantic 6-3389 . . . in Pittsburgh. Pittsburgh, P A.

(*Blackout*)

SHERIFF'S OFFICE

Lights rise swiftly. CARSON *sits near desk, writing on small note-pad. The clock reads 5:32.* BARD *is finishing a telephone conversation, a note of exultation in his voice.*

BARD

(*Into phone*)

Yeah . . . okay . . . good deal! (*He replaces the phone*) Pittsburgh! They've located Helen Laski. Avalon Hotel, Pittsburgh. We'll have a record of any calls to or from . . . in a few minutes now.

CARSON

Bard . . . stop me if I'm out of line . . . but what's this thing to you? You, personally?

BARD

(*Slowly rubbing his chin*)
You've heard of that first law of the jungle . . . haven't you,
Carson? (*The light on the radio flashes.* BARD *presses the button, snaps*) Deputy Bard!

WINSTON'S VOICE

Jess . . . this is Winston. Car three.

BARD

What've you got, Tom?

WINSTON'S VOICE

That hardware store holdup on the south side . . .

BARD

(*Eagerly*)
Yeah? Yeah?

WINSTON'S VOICE

(*Wearily*)
No guns stolen. All they took was fishing rods.
(BARD *presses the button and looks at* CARSON.)

CARSON

They'd be too shrewd to pull a stunt like that.

BARD

Look, Carson . . . do me a favor. It's almost time for supper. All I've heard since morning is how damn wise those
rats are. I'm up to here with it.

CARSON

Where're they getting their clothes?

BARD

My theory is they're running around naked so nobody'll
notice 'em. (*The telephone rings.* BARD *picks it up*) Deputy

27

Bard . . . Yeah . . . (*Disappointment*) Yeah. Okay. (*Hangs up*) Helen Laski checked out of the Avalon Hotel last night. No phone calls, no messages of any kind received today. . . . (CARSON *rises and with a look at* BARD *goes to the window.* BARD *bursts out*) I know! I know! They'd be too smart to make a call to a hotel. They used somebody in between!

CARSON

(*At the window*)

I didn't say a word.

BARD

You know where that leaves us, don't you? Beating our tails ragged over nothing around here.

CARSON

Only you don't believe it.

BARD

Sure I believe it. I'm a trained police officer. I go by the facts, not crazy hunches. I reckon they're not here.

CARSON

(*Turns*)

Why don't you put some more patrol cars on the streets, anyway? Just in case?

BARD

(*Rises and paces*)

That damn jalopy's been reported in every state in the union . . . sixty times in Indiana alone! The earth won't open up and swallow it! Okay, let's try anything! (*He picks up phone, dials . . . as the lights dim*) Where is that beat-up gray car?

HILLIARD HOME

*It is dark outside and dim throughout the house,
except for the living room which is brilliantly lighted.*
ELEANOR *sits on the sofa, staring ahead.* HANK *is in the
pantry sitting in a chair which is obviously from the
breakfast nook; he holds the portable radio from*
RALPHIE'S *room in his lap with the music playing—
a loud jazzy tune, in contrast to the soft gentleness of
the morning music.* HANK *wears a dark red shirt with
a cardigan sweater over it and the prison trousers. He
smokes fairly steadily.*

*The ravages of the afternoon are everywhere ap-
parent; the atmosphere of invasion hangs over the
entire house. There is an open box of cigars on the
coffee table with some of the cigars scattered on the
table. There is a carton of cigarettes, with the top
ripped back, on the table. A coffee cup is also on the
table and another is on the table beside the armchair.
There are odds and ends of food. The ashtrays are
filled to overflowing.*

In the living room, GLENN, *at window, is filled with
a sense of triumph; he is almost gay, and his enjoy-
ment of what follows is clear.* GLENN *wears a pair of*
DAN'S *slacks and a sport shirt.* ELEANOR, *alert in every
fiber, is pale, haggard, stiff.* ROBISH *is entering from
the den; he is wearing a full suit including shirt and
tie—*DAN'S *best, and it does not quite fit. A cigar is
jammed in the corner of his mouth.*

ROBISH

What if this joker gets suspicious . . . that gray car parked
right in his own garage?

GLENN
(*Casually*)

Can it, Robish.

ROBISH

(*To* ELEANOR)

Why ain't he here? You said quarter to six.

ELEANOR

The traffic may be heavy . . . or Cindy may have had to
work late . . . or . . . anything . . . *anything!*

(HANK *suddenly rises and looks out the window in
the side door. He moves up toward the kitchen door
and calls:*)

HANK

Glenn! Black coop just turned in the driveway.

GLENN

Turn off the clatter back there, Hank.

(HANK *turns off the radio and places it on the back
stairs.*)

HANK

(*Looking out the side door*)

You want me to grab 'em?

GLENN

Not with all them cars goin' by out there.

HANK

Woman comin' around to the front door, Glenn.

(ELEANOR *places her hand at her mouth.* GLENN *unlocks the door.*)

GLENN

(*To* ELEANOR)

You don't have to do nothin' but keep your trap shut. (*He
turns the gun to cover the front door. There is a brief pause.
The front door opens and* CINDY *enters, casually, swiftly, a*

trifle breathless. She stops dead when she sees GLENN) Come right in, redhead. (CINDY *backs away, pulling the door closed, but she suddenly stops, frozen in the door. The reason she stops is simply that* GLENN *has turned the gun toward* ELEANOR's *head*) We still got the old lady, Sis. (ROBISH *is standing at den door . . . dull, brutish . . . with his little eyes roving over* CINDY. CINDY *closes the door and stands in front of it.* GLENN *grins*) That's bein' real sensible.

CINDY
(*Planting her feet slightly*)
Mother . . . how long have these animals been here?
(ELEANOR *starts, as though she would warn* CINDY. GLENN's *grin flickers, fades and a hardness comes into his face . . . but not into his tone.*)

GLENN
Spitfire, too. You watch out, redhead.

HANK
(*At side door, calls*)
Glenn! He's lookin' in the garage.

GLENN
(*Calling to* HANK—*confident, knowing*)
He'll come in. (*He grabs* CINDY *and pushes her toward chair*) Sit down now, sweetie . . . and no talking. Not a goddam word.

HANK
(*In pantry*)
He's coming around now—fast.
(GLENN *moves into position near front door. Pause. Then the door opens, and* DAN *enters, evening paper in hand.*)

31

DAN

Ellie, whose car is that in the . . .
(GLENN *slams door shut behind* DAN, *and* DAN *breaks off, staring in bewilderment at* GLENN, *then at the gun.*)

GLENN
(*In flat cold tones*)
It's loaded. Now lock the door. . . . (*Sardonically*) Please.
(*Unable to speak yet, his eyes on* GLENN, DAN *turns and locks the door. Then:*)

DAN
(*Baffled; softly*)
What're you . . . why . . . I don't . . .

GLENN

You never know what's comin', do you, Pop?
(DAN *then turns to* ELEANOR.)

DAN

Ellie? . . .

ELEANOR

I'm all right, Dan.

DAN
(*Looking about the room, glances toward stairs*)
Where's Ralphie?

ELEANOR

Not home yet.

HANK
(*Calls from pantry*)
Driveway ain't blocked, Glenn.

CINDY

The house is crawling with them, Dad.

GLENN

(*Sizing her up*)
Don't get me jumpy, redhead, this things liable to explode.

DAN

(*Flatly, glancing at newspaper in his hand*)
Glenn Griffin.

GLENN

(*Laughs, takes paper*)
Lotsa people heard-a me, didn't they? (*In satisfaction*)
Front page. (*Disgusted*) They always gotta use the same god-
dam picture.
(*He tosses the paper to the floor.*)

DAN

Griffin . . . you fire that thing . . . and you'll have the whole
neighborhood in here in two minutes.

GLENN

I don't want to take that chance, Hilliard . . . any more'n
you want me to.

ROBISH

You dumb, mister?

GLENN

(*Sizing up* DAN)
Naw, he ain't dumb, Robish. He's a smart-eyed bastard,
this guy. . . .

DAN

What're you . . . I don't understand . . . what do you *want?*

GLENN

Take it easy, Pop.

33

DAN

(*Controlling himself with effort*)
What do you want here?

GLENN

(*Takes a step toward* DAN)
I don't want nobody to get hurt. . . . What do *you* want,
Pop?

DAN

That's . . . what I want, too. (*Then, shrewdly*) That's what
you're depending on, isn't it?

GLENN

You got it, Buster. First try.

DAN

But . . . why *here?* Why *my* house?

GLENN

Your break, Pop. I like the location. Those empty lots'n
both sides. The bike parked on the nice lawn. I like suckers
with kids . . . they don't take no chances.

DAN

Anyone who could think up a scheme like that is . . .

GLENN

(*Cutting in*)
. . . is smart, Pop.

ELEANOR

(*Quickly*)
Dan! They've done nothing.

34

GLENN

Now I'm gonna explain the facts-a-life to you, Hilliard. You listen, too, redhead . . . listen good. You can get brave . . . any one of you . . . just about any time you feel up to it. Might even get away with it. *But* . . . that ain't sayin' what'll happen to the others . . . the old lady here . . . the redhead . . . the little guy owns the bike. . . . (*Slight pause*) Okay, Pop, you got it all the way now.

(*Another pause.* DAN *moves to sofa and drops his hat on it.* ELEANOR's *hand and his meet, briefly clasping.* DAN *turns to* GLENN.)

DAN
(*Taking a deep breath*)
How long?

GLENN
(*Grinning*)
Now that's the kinda sensible talk a guy likes to hear.

DAN
(*Firmly*)
How long?

GLENN

Matter of hours . . . before midnight . . . maybe sooner. Meantime, everything goes on just like normal.

DAN

Why midnight?

GLENN
(*Almost politely*)
None-a your goddam business.

ELEANOR

They have a friend coming . . . with money.

35

DAN

What if . . .

GLENN

(*Speaking at the same time; stops* DAN)
Lady, you speak when I tell you.

DAN

The police are looking everywhere for you. What if . . .

GLENN

They ain't looking here, Pop. They show here, it ain't
gonna be pretty.

DAN

They could trail your friend . . .

GLENN

Let's get one thing straight, Pop. (*Gesturing to the window*) Any red lights show out there . . . you folks get it first.
(*There is a slight pause.* DAN *crosses to the window and peeks
out between the drawn curtains.* GLENN *laughs*) Gives you a
funny feelin', don't it? You don't know what's happenin' . . .
or where . . . or what it adds up to . . . for you. Ever had that
feelin' before, Pop? Me, I get it all the time. Even kinda like
it. But you and me . . . we ain't much alike, are we, Pop?

CINDY

(*A breath*)
Thank God.

DAN

(*Turns from window*)
Griffin . . . if you . . . what if I could get you the same
amount of money you're waiting for? Now. Before midnight.

ROBISH

Hey, that don't sound like a bad . . .

GLENN

Hilliard, you maybe think you're a big shot . . . fifteen thousand a year. But I had me a look at your bankbooks. Two hundred lousy bucks in the kitty. Hell, I had more'n fifteen grand in my hands at one time, Pop . . . and I ain't twenty-five yet.

CINDY

I hope it helped pass your time in jail . . . counting it.

DAN

I could raise more. I could . . .

ROBISH

What about that? We could blow outta here right away! This joker's usin' his brain.

GLENN

(Sharply)

Use yours, Robish. Helen's on her way *here*.

ROBISH

To hell with that! Why should me and the kid risk our necks . . . just so you can get some copper knocked off.

GLENN

(Dangerously now—low and intense)

Go spill your guts somewhere else!

ROBISH

(Shouting)

What do I care who busted your goddam jawbone?

GLENN

(Topping him)

I'll bust yours if . . .

(They are now shouting at each other across DAN.)

37

ROBISH

This guy talks sense! Don't I have nothin' to say? . . .

GLENN

NO! You ain't got a goddam stinkin' thing to say! (ROBISH *retreats slightly.* GLENN *turns on* DAN *more quietly but with force*) You, Hilliard . . . I seen what you been up to. Robish here, he ain't got a brain. *But* . . . he ain't got a gun, either. Don't try to get in between, you smart-eyed sonofabitch. Clickety-clickety-click. (*He makes a gesture at* DAN's *temple*) I can see them wheels goin' around in there, Pop. *Don't ever try that again!* (*He backs away, eyes on* DAN; *speaks softly now—to* ELEANOR) Now, lady . . . serve us up that chicken you been thawin' out.

DAN

My wife's not your servant.

GLENN

(*Thinly . . . daring* DAN *to protest*)
I always wanted me a servant. . . .

ELEANOR

(*Begins to rise*)
I don't mind, Dan.

DAN

(*Firmly*)
I do. Sit down, Ellie.

GLENN

(*Exploding wildly*)
Lissen, Hilliard! I . . . (*Then he stops; sizing* DAN *up, forcing control . . . almost quietly at first, building in intensity*) I had a old man like you. Always callin' the tune. Outside his house, nobody. Inside, Mister God! Little punk went to church every Sunday . . . took it from everybody . . . licked

their shoes . . . tried to beat it into Hank'n me . . . be a punk, be a nobody . . . take it from you shiny-shoed, down-your-noses sonsabitches with white handkerchiefs in your pockets! (*He snatches the handkerchief from* DAN's *breast pocket, spits into it, and throws it on the floor*) You remember, Pop . . . I could kill you just for kicks. (*Pause. Without taking his eyes off* DAN *he again gestures to* ELEANOR, *speaks coldly again*) Now, lady . . . get out there'n cook it.

(ELEANOR *starts to rise, but* HANK's *voice stops her.*)

HANK

(*Turning from window in side door*)
Kid comin' up the driveway . . . walkin' . . .
(GLENN *starts for the front door.*)

DAN

Griffin . . . you've got to let me explain to Ralphie first. . . .
(ROBISH *grabs* DAN *by the shoulders and shoves him against the window.*)

GLENN

I don't got to do nothin'. You pull anything now, you can sit'n watch me kick the kid's face in.

HANK

(*Calling again from the side door*)
Comin' to the front door . . .

GLENN

(*At front door, unlocks it*)
You got to learn to take orders from other people now, Pop. . . .
(*The front door opens and* RALPHIE *enters, whistling.* GLENN *slams the door behind him and locks it.* RALPHIE *stops.*)

39

RALPHIE

(*Bewildered*)

Hey . . . what is . . . (ROBISH *takes a single step*) Who are you? (*He turns to the door, sees* GLENN. *A split second. Then he turns and runs to the dining room . . . as* HANK *appears in the dining-room door*) Get out of . . .

(RALPHIE *whirls and dashes to the front door, evading* GLENN.)

DAN

(*Quickly*)

Ralphie, it's all right! It's . . .

(ROBISH *grabs* RALPHIE *at the door. He shakes him by the shoulders roughly, venting on the child the spleen that* GLENN *has stirred in him.*)

ROBISH

Where ya think you're goin? Don't you know who's boss 'roun' here? Ya gotta take orders from Griffin. Griffin's the big shot 'roun' here. . . .

(*As* RALPHIE'S *head snaps back and forth,* DAN *moves. He grabs* ROBISH, *whips him around.* RALPHIE *breaks away and runs, fighting tears, to* ELEANOR *on the sofa. She takes him in her arms as he sits, clutching her.* DAN *slams* ROBISH *against the window and draws back for a blow, his mind gone blank; he is propelled blindly by jungle atavistic urges beyond his control. But* GLENN *steps in.*)

GLENN

It ain't gonna be like this! Not like this, see! (*In the scuffle the table near the chair is overturned.* ELEANOR *stifles a scream as* GLENN *brings the gun down on* DAN's *shoulder.* DAN *goes down.* ROBISH *recovers and starts toward* DAN, *but* GLENN *steps in between*) You hear me, Robish? *Nothin's gonna screw this up!*

ROBISH

(*Blinking owlishly at the gun in* GLENN's *hand*)
You think I'm gonna let that . . .

GLENN

(*An order—low, intense*)
Get outta here!

ROBISH

(*Glaring, goes to dining-room door*)
My gut's growlin' again.
  (ROBISH *kicks open the dining-room door and exits.*
  DAN, *his tie askew, manages to sit in chair, holding his*
  shoulder. GLENN *regains his familiar swagger.*)

GLENN

Give the old lady a hand, redhead. Out there . . . if you
please.
  (CINDY *and* ELEANOR *rise,* ELEANOR *going into dining*
  room.)

CINDY

Where do we keep the rat poison?
  (*As* CINDY *follows* ELEANOR, HANK *steps into her path,*
  blocking her way. GLENN *laughs and crosses to foot of*
  stairs; CINDY *is trapped between them.*)

GLENN
(*Goading* DAN)
She's a honey, ain't she, Hank?

HANK
(*Arrogantly*)
I don't go for redheads.

DAN
(*Sensing danger for* CINDY)
Griffin . . .

41

CINDY

(*With a sharpness, to* HANK)
For God's small favors, make me eternally grateful.
(HANK *drops his arm and* CINDY *exits into the dining
room.* HANK *follows her with his eyes and gives a low
whistle.* GLENN *turns to* DAN.)

GLENN

Kid's been in stir for three years, Pop. Don't cost nothin'
to look.

DAN

(*His eyes still on* HANK)
Just don't try changing your mind, young fellow.

GLENN

Hilliard, you're a funny gink. You don't know when you're
licked, do you? . . . Now just one thing—you got a gun in the
house?

RALPHIE

(*Too quickly, as he kneels on sofa*)
No . . . we don't.

GLENN

(*Enjoying himself*)
Well, Pop?

DAN

You heard the boy. I don't have a gun.

GLENN

That's right. You don't. Show him, Hank. (*After* HANK *dis-
plays the automatic*) There for a minute I thought you was
gonna lie to me, Pop.

DAN

Griffin . . . listen to me . . .

42

GLENN

I'll do the talkin'. You listen, Hilliard! That dough's half-way here now and nothin's gonna foul this up, see. You pull any of that muscle-stuff again . . .

DAN

That won't happen again . . .

GLENN

. . . and I'm gonna let Robish work you over . . .

DAN

. . . I went blank there for a . . .

GLENN

. . . after that, you ain't gonna know what happens to the others. That the way you want it?

DAN

Griffin . . . (*Very softly . . . with strength now*) *hands off.*

GLENN

I don't go for threats. . . .

DAN

Hands off, that's all I know! If one of you touches one of us again . . .

GLENN

Don't talk tough to me, Hilliard. . . .

DAN

. . . I can't promise what'll happen. . . . I can't promise *any-thing* . . . if one of you touches one of us again. I don't *know* what I'll do. Can't you understand that, you half-baked squirt? I'll make you use that gun, Griffin. So help me. We're

43

done for then, but so are you. (*Drops voice*) It won't matter then whether your friend gets here or not. . . .

(*Blackout*)

SHERIFF'S OFFICE

The clock reads 7:03. WINSTON, *his feet propped up on desk, is trying to sleep. The radio signal is flickering.* BARD *flips on radio.*

CARSON'S VOICE

Bard . . . this is Carson.

BARD
(*Wearily*)

I'm still here, Carson.

CARSON'S VOICE

Helen Laski's been spotted.

BARD
(*Changing—alert and eager*)

Where?

CARSON'S VOICE

She's heading west from Pittsburgh. On U.S. 40. Driving very slow and careful. Approaching Columbus, Ohio. Heading west!

BARD
(*With satisfaction*)

West!

CARSON'S VOICE

Ought to be here about eleven or twelve tonight.

BARD
(*An excited throb in his voice*)

Okay. Now listen. Don't let anyone tail her. I don't want her picked up, or alerted. But I want her clocked. Every town she goes through . . . every village. I want to know every time she stops to get gas, go to the can, anything.

CARSON'S VOICE

Looks like your hunch is paying off, Bard.

BARD

Could be, Carson. *Could be!* (BARD *flips off the radio and slaps* WINSTON's *feet off the desk*) I told you they were homing pigeons, Tom! They do it every time . . . right back to the womb that spewed 'em.

WINSTON

Okay, they're pigeons. You're an owl. I'm sleepy.

BARD

They're layin' low here now . . . thinkin' how clever they been . . . getting Laski out of town so she could backtrack to 'em. Clever! *Not so damned!*

WINSTON

Jess, you're raving. How long since you ate solid food?

DUTCH'S VOICE
(*On intercom*)

Jess . . .

BARD
(*Flips intercom button*)

Yeah, Dutch?

DUTCH'S VOICE

Your wife called again. She says she's still at your mother's but drowning in a sea of words . . . whatever that means.

45

BARD
(With a laugh)
Tell her to stay there all night, Dutch. Tell her I said it's
. . . uh . . . Be-Kind-to-Talkative-Mothers-Week. (*He flips off
the intercom, turns to* WINSTON *exultantly*) About twenty
miles out of town, we'll put a real tag on Miss Helen Laski
and she'll breeze right in and lead us straight to the hole!
How many hours till midnight, Tom?

WINSTON
By my watch . . . (*The lights begin to dim*) too god-
damned-many.

(Blackout)

HILLIARD HOME

*The living room lights are on; the rest of the house
is in dimness.* HANK *is in the chair in the pantry, smoking. In the living room the family is arranged in a pat-
tern within view of the windows. The curtains are
slightly open.* ROBISH *is sitting on the stairs.* GLENN *is
lounging in a chair near the windows.* DAN *looks at his
watch.*

GLENN
Pop, that's a good-looking timepiece you got there. (*He
extends his hand*) I'll take it. (DAN *rises, pauses . . . then slips
the wrist-watch band off his wrist. He crosses and hands the
watch to* GLENN, *who examines it*) Fancy. (*He slips it on his
own wrist*) D'you snitch this from that department store,
Pop?

DAN
(Quietly . . . with dignity)
My wife gave it to me . . . on our twentieth anniversary.
(He returns to sit.)

46

GLENN

(*Winding the watch*)

Now ain't that real touchin'? (*To* RALPHIE) Hey, Buster ...
ain't it time for you to hit the sack? You want to grow up, be
a big man like Pop here, don't you?

> (RALPHIE *kisses* ELEANOR *good-night, then crosses directly to* GLENN.)

RALPHIE

Half-baked squirt!

> (ROBISH *laughs.* GLENN *grabs the front of* RALPHIE'S
> *shirt but releases him after a moment with a laugh.*
> RALPHIE *turns and goes upstairs and into his own
> room and sits on the bed.*)

GLENN

(*As* RALPHIE *goes*)

Some brat you got there, missus. Some day he's gonna get
his head knocked off.

> (DAN *rises and crosses to the stairs.* ROBISH *stands up
> and blocks his way.*)

ROBISH

What you think you're gonna do ... go to the toilet for
him?

GLENN

It's his house, Robish. Hilliard don't want that kid holler-
ing out a window up there any more'n we do. (ROBISH *steps
down from the stairs and* DAN *goes up to* RALPHIE'S *room.*
ROBISH *moves toward the window.* GLENN *flips off the living-
room lights and jumps up, closing the window curtains*) How
many times I gotta tell you—stay outta the way-a them windows! (*He motions* ROBISH *toward the den*) Get in there and
turn on the television.

47

ROBISH
(*Protesting*)

Listen, Griffin . . .

GLENN

And keep it lit so it looks natural from out front.
(ROBISH *stomps angrily into the den. The living room is now in dimness.* DAN *turns on light in* RALPHIE'S *room, stands a moment without speaking.* RALPHIE *studies his father a second.*)

RALPHIE

Dad . . . they're not so tough.

DAN
(*Still facing the door, abstracted*)

Don't you fool yourself, Ralphie.

RALPHIE

You could've licked the big guy if that Griffin hadn't . . .

DAN
(*Turning to the boy*)

Ralphie, we can't lick them . . . at least not that way. I lost my temper, that's all. I . . . can't let that happen again.

RALPHIE
(*Not daring to believe it*)

Dad . . . are you scared?

DAN

Of course not. Why, you ought to know . . . (*He suddenly sits on the bed, facing the boy*) Ralphie, listen to me. Those two guns they have down there . . . they're loaded. Those are real bullets. When a gun goes off, it doesn't only make a sound. Those bullets can kill people. Do you understand that, son?

48

RALPHIE

I've been thinking . . . I could climb out Cindy's window . . . out across the porch roof. . . . I could get to the Wallings. Get help . . .

DAN

(Patience running thin)

Ralphie . . .

RALPHIE

The porch isn't much higher'n the garage roof. I've jumped off the garage roof a lot of times.

DAN

Ralphie, how many times have I told you to stay off the garage roof?

RALPHIE

You could, though. I'll *bet* you could.

DAN

Look, Ralphie . . . Listen, Ralph . . . Ralph. You want me to call you Ralph, don't you? You want to be considered a grown-up boy in this house? Then you've got to behave like one . . . *think* like one . . . beginning right now!

RALPHIE

I've got a better idea. I could wait till that young one goes into the living room, sometime, then sneak down the back stairs. . . .

DAN

(Anger rising)

Ralphie, didn't you hear them? If you got out of here . . . even if you brought the police . . . do you know what would happen? They would shoot your mother and your sister . . . and *you* . . . *you'd* be the reason they did it.

49

RALPHIE

You *are* scared.

DAN

No, no, of course not . . . It's only . . . (*Suddenly changes*) Yes, son . . . yes, I'm scared. But I'm not ashamed of being scared. . . . Sometimes it's better to be scared. You think about that now. You think hard about that, hear?

RALPHIE

Well, I'm not. And Cindy's not either.

DAN
(*Rising, urgently*)

You'd better . . .

(*The telephone in the house rings.* DAN *stops. Immediate tension . . . there is a pause until the second ring starts.* GLENN *rises and turns on the living-room lights.* HANK *runs up the back stairs and to the phone extension in the upstairs hall.* ROBISH *appears in the door of the den.*)

GLENN

Hank! (*To* CINDY) Okay, redhead . . . you get the pleasure. (CINDY *rises from the sofa and crosses toward telephone*) If it's for Mr. James, I'll take it. Anyone else, let 'em talk . . . except the brat.

(*The telephone continues to ring—insistently, mechanically.* HANK *picks up the phone in the upstairs hall with his hand on the circuit breaker in the cradle until he hears* CINDY *speak. Then he opens the circuit and listens.* DAN *stands behind the door to* RALPHIE'S *room . . . alert, waiting.*)

HANK
(*When he is ready at the phone*)

Okay, Glenn.

50

GLENN

(*Beside* CINDY *at the phone table*)

Like any other night, see. Normal.

(CINDY *picks up the phone with her left hand.* GLENN *grabs the instrument and puts it in her right hand so he can try to listen, too.*)

CINDY

(*Into phone*)

Hello? . . . Oh . . . No, I can't . . . not tonight . . . I simply can't, that's all. . . . Nothing's the matter, I . . .

(*She slowly replaces the phone. Upstairs,* HANK *replaces the extension and starts down the stairs into the living room.* DAN *opens the door of* RALPHIE'S *room and comes down a few steps on the stairs.*)

GLENN

(*To* CINDY—*impatiently*)

Well? *Well?*

CINDY

(*Bleakly*)

I flunked.

GLENN

Who was it?

HANK

(*Descending stairs*)

His name's Chuck. And he's coming, anyway. For a date.

(*Pause* . . . HANK'S *eyes on* CINDY. GLENN *takes a few steps, thinking furiously.*)

GLENN

You ain't 's wise's I thought you was, spitfire.

HANK

She couldn't help it. He was in a drug store around the corner. Wouldn't even listen. Wants her to go dancing.

GLENN

(*Turns to* CINDY)

Okay. You be ready, cutie. When boy friend stops out front, you duck out. . . .

(*Pause: general amazement.*)

ROBISH

Griffin . . . you off your rocker?

GLENN

(*Calling*)

Hilliard . . . get down here. (*To* ELEANOR) You stick with the brat, he don't get ideas.

(ELEANOR *rises and starts up the stairs, passing* DAN *as he descends.*)

DAN

(*To* ELEANOR, *in a low voice*)

Lock the door.

(GLENN *flips on radio, then crosses to* CINDY *as the music rises.*)

GLENN

You wanna dance, redhead? You should-a told Hank. (*To* HANK) C'mon, kid, you want a dance, take a dance. (*To* CINDY, *who moves slightly away*) Give the kid a break, spitfire.

(DAN *watches tensely . . . as* HANK *looks* CINDY *over, with arrogance, but the longing clear in his face. Then* HANK *moves, crossing toward* CINDY, *passing her, flipping off the radio. In silence, he walks with dignity, inwardly disturbed, toward the dining-room door, exits.*)

52

A moment—while GLENN *stares after* HANK, *amazed, frowning. Above,* ELEANOR *enters* RALPHIE's *bedroom, closes and locks door, turns off bedroom light.)*

GLENN
(Baffled, almost to himself)
Oughta see Hank dance. Has all the babes groggy.
(HANK *appears in pantry, oddly shaken.*)

HANK
(In whisper)
Dammitohell . . .

GLENN
(Recovering, turning to DAN)
Hilliard . . . the gas is low in that fancy buggy of yours.
Fill'er up'n check the battery'n oil.

ROBISH
You ain't lettin' 'em *both* out?
(In the pantry, HANK *sinks into the chair, sits quietly.*)

GLENN
The kid'n the missus stay. Him or the redhead pull something, they know what'll happen here. Pop here's a smart cookie. He don't want no coppers settin' up machine guns on his nice smooth lawn . . . throwin' tear gas through his windows. *(Moves closer to* DAN, *threateningly)* Cause that happens, you know who's gonna get it, don't you, Hilliard? Not you. *(He gestures upstairs) Them.* I'm gonna see to it personal. *(Slowly)* An' you're gonna stay alive to remember it the rest of your life.
(There is a pause. Then DAN *steps toward* CINDY.)

DAN
You hear that, Cindy?
(DAN *crosses to closet and gets his coat and* CINDY's.)

53

CINDY

I'll do *anything* to get away from that voice.

ROBISH

Okay, everybody's gone nuts. Gimme some liquor.

DAN

No, no liquor.

GLENN

This time the old man's right, Robish.

ROBISH

(*Shrewdly—striking the weak spot*)
You lettin' this joker give the orders?

GLENN

(*Tricked*)
Nobody gives me orders. Not ever again! (*To* DAN) Make it bourbon, Pop. Bonded. (*To* CINDY) You . . . bring back some late-edition papers.
(*He sits.*)

CINDY

(*Getting into her coat—scathingly*)
Would you like a scrapbook and a jar of paste?
(HANK, *suddenly alert in pantry, looks out window of side door.*)

HANK

(*Calling*)
Car stoppin' at the curb. Little low-slung job. Foreign make, some kind.

CINDY

(*To* GLENN)
It's a Jaguar. You should know what a jaguar is . . . it's a fierce jungle animal . . . very brave against smaller, less

ferocious animals. But it's a snarling coward when trapped. (*She goes to the door.* DAN *follows, stops her.*)

DAN

Cindy! (*She turns to him; slight pause; then gently*) You . . . you be careful, hear?
(*As* DAN *opens the door,* GLENN *rises quickly and steps to the dining-room door, out of sight of the front door.* CINDY *goes out and* DAN *closes the door.* HANK *watches out the window of the side door.*)

GLENN

If that spitfire tries anything!

DAN

Griffin . . . what if the police track you down? Sooner or later . . . through no fault of ours . . . what if . . .

GLENN

(*Smugly—in control*)
I'd never know who done it, Pop.

DAN

But you couldn't blame *us!*

GLENN

(*Slowly*)
Hilliard, I got news for you. I—can—do—anything—I—want. Nice family you got here, Pop. You love that woman of yours, you ain't gonna reach for no phone in that filling station. Them coppers're after *me,* y'know. They don't give a hoot in hell about you. *Or* your family. (*He crosses to the door*) Clickety-clickety-click . . . give you something to think about, Pop.
(GLENN *opens the door and gestures* DAN *to go.* DAN *goes out, setting his shoulders. Above,* ELEANOR *watches out* RALPHIE's *window.*)

ROBISH

(*As* GLENN *closes and locks the door*)
Jeez, I'm gettin' up a thirst all of a sudden.
(*He exits into den.* GLENN, *after a short pause, turns out the living-room lights and goes through the dining-room door and into the pantry where he joins* HANK, *who stares moodily out the window of the side door.*)

GLENN

Kid, everythin's chimin'! Told you I'd shack you up in style, didn't I?

HANK

(*Noncommital*)
Yeah ...

GLENN

Hey ... what's eatin' you, anyway?

HANK

Y'know something, Glenn? I never had a "date" in my life.

GLENN

Date? Hell, you laid enough babes to ...

HANK

Naw, I mean a *date*. Y'know ... ordinary things like that.

GLENN

(*Scornfully*)
Malted milks? Hot dogs at a drive-in?

HANK

Maybe ...

GLENN

You got it comin', kid . . . all the babes you can handle and still walk straight up.

HANK

Babes like Helen?

GLENN
(*Astonished*)
Yeah. . . . What's the matter with Helen?

HANK

She's a tramp.
(HANK *goes to the kitchen door and disappears.* GLENN *stares after him, puzzled.*)

(*Blackout*)

SHERIFF'S OFFICE
BARD *is at the desk, working over various reports.* CARSON *enters briskly. Clock: 8:56.*

CARSON

Bard . . . hold onto your hat. She's not coming.

BARD

What're you talking about . . . not coming? She's half-way . . .

CARSON
(*Shaking his head*)
Helen Laski's not coming. She made one simple mistake. She ran a red light on the outskirts of Columbus. A patrol car gave chase.

BARD

(Rising, outraged)

Carson . . . are you telling me they arrested Helen Laski for a traffic violation? Good God, they had orders! It's been on every teletype for hours . . . *do not arrest!*

CARSON

They didn't arrest her. She gave them the slip . . . in downtown Columbus. Abandoned the convertible. Swallowed up. Presto! *(He shrugs)* These mistakes are bound to happen.

BARD

You can't afford mistakes against a mind like Glenn Griffin's! *(He sits at the desk and flips the button on the intercom)* Dutch! I want every long distance telephone call and a record of very telegram from Columbus, Ohio, to Indianapolis from . . .

(He looks at CARSON.)

CARSON

Eight.

BARD

From eight o'clock to now . . . and straight through the night. As fast as they get 'em. Any number to any number. Names, addresses, the works. *(Flips off the intercom, sits back)* Imagine those greedy sonsabitches in Columbus trying to pick her off for a lousy fifteen-buck fine!

CARSON

(Sits and picks up the deck of cards on the desk)

She has to contact him . . . wherever he is. All we can do is wait. How about a game of double solitaire?

BARD
(Rising and pacing)
Wait ... wait ... wait.

(Dimout)

HILLIARD HOME

The lights are dim throughout the house. ELEANOR *is moving from the window to the door in* RALPHIE'S *room.* RALPHIE *is asleep on his bed.* HANK *is in the pantry watching out the window of the side door.* ROBISH *is turning from the window in the living room.*

GLENN *is leaving the pantry to appear in the living room.*

ROBISH
Tired-awaitin'. I been thinkin' about a snort of whisky for eighteen years.

GLENN
(As he enters from the dining room)
Shut up, he's comin' in. *(He gestures for* ROBISH *to turn on the living-room lights.* ROBISH *turns on the lights and unlocks and opens the front door.* DAN *enters, the fury and frustration packed solid through his whole frame. A new fear has taken root in him now, and he speaks flatly, quietly.* GLENN *says:)* C'mere, Pop. *(As* DAN *crosses and* ROBISH *closes and locks the front door)* You mind takin' your hands outta your pockets? *(*DAN *obliges)* Thank you kindly. . . .

ROBISH
Where the hell you been?
*(*DAN *faces* ROBISH. GLENN *frisks him expertly.)*

DAN
The service stations close early in this neighborhood. . . . *(*GLENN *is circling* DAN*)* I don't have a gun, Griffin.

59

(GLENN *brings the whisky bottle out of* DAN's *coat pocket. It is in a paper bag which he removes and drops on the floor.*)

ROBISH
(*Outraged, seeing the bottle*)
Chrissake, a pint!

DAN
You didn't specify any particular amount.

GLENN
(*Laughs, looking at the bottle*)
Kentucky Tavern . . . nothing but the best for Pop! (*As* ROBISH *snatches the bottle*) Robish, go'n out'n check the car over.
(*He sits on the sofa, putting his feet up.*)

ROBISH
(*Working with the bottle*)
Maybe he's got coppers stashed in the back seat. Let Hank check it.

GLENN
(*Dismissing it—lifts voice*)
Hank! Check the car.

HANK
(*Bitterly*)
Yeh . . . me. (*He rises from the chair and opens the door as he calls*) Okay, Glenn.
(*He exits through the side door, closing it.* DAN *goes to the stairs, begins to mount.*)

GLENN
You didn't get any ideas out there, did you, Hilliard?

ROBISH

(*Struggling with bottle*)

Kee-rist . . . eighteen years an' then you can't get it open!
(*Succeeds, takes a long swig from bottle.*)

DAN

(*On second step of stairs, calls*)

Ellie . . .

ELEANOR

(*Comes out of the room to the head of the stairs*)
We're all right, Dan. Cindy's not back yet.

GLENN

Pop, when I ask you a question, you answer!

DAN

(*Turns, flatly*)

No. No ideas.
(*Above,* ELEANOR *returns to* RALPHIE'S *room and closes
the door.* HANK *re-enters the pantry and speaks as he
crosses toward the living room.*)

HANK

Car's okay. (*He enters the living room through the dining-
room door*) I didn't try the motor. (*A glance at* DAN) Looks
like the whole street's gone to sleep.

GLENN

See, Robish. Hank ain't yellow. Taught him how not to be
yellow, didn't I, Hank?

HANK

You taught me everything.
(*The strange twist of bitterness in his tone causes*
GLENN *to look at him sharply.*)

61

DAN
(*Haunted by his new fear*)
Griffin . . .

GLENN
(*Briskly; unpleasantly now*)
Your woman's waitin'. Go to bed.

DAN
(*Firmly*)
Griffin . . . when you do leave tonight, we're staying in this house. My family. All of us.

GLENN
(*Eyes on* HANK)
Yeh, yeh. You give me a fair shake, I give you a fair shake. (*Pause.* DAN *stands, thinking.* HANK *crosses to take the bottle from* ROBISH; *drinks.* GLENN *rises, glaring at* DAN. DAN *turns and goes upstairs.* GLENN *stops* HANK *as he returns the bottle to* ROBISH *and turns to leave the room.* GLENN *presses on, puzzled*) I did teach you everything, didn't I, Hank?

HANK
(*Meeting his brother's gaze: levelly*)
Yeh. Everything . . . except maybe how to live in a house like this.
(HANK *goes swiftly to dining-room door and exits. He enters the pantry and sits in the chair. Above,* DAN *enters the master bedroom, takes off topcoat, and sits in the dimness on the bed, facing the door, alone.* GLENN, *after a pause, follows* HANK *into the pantry.*)

ROBISH
Ahhh . . . my gut's beginnin' to burn good!
(ROBISH *turns off the living-room lights, then sits, drinking.*)

GLENN
(*In the pantry; baffled*)
Live here? We ain't gonna *live* here.

HANK
No. Or any place like it. Ever.

GLENN
Hank, what the hell's . . .

HANK
When Helen gets here, we gonna give Hilliard a fair shake?

GLENN
(*Angrily*)
Anybody ever give *you* a fair shake?

HANK
Who the hell ever had a chance?

GLENN
(*An idea*)
The redhead! She got you goin', kid? (*Laughs and kneels facing* HANK; *with warm comradeship*) Tell you what, kid . . . when we leave, we'll take her along. Just for you.

HANK
(*After a pause—bitterly*)
Fair shake!

GLENN
(*Anger again*)
What you think I'm gonna do? (*Trying to sell* HANK *the idea*) Nobody's gonna be suspicious if we got two women'n the car. We'll take 'em both. (*He gives* HANK *a playful punch*) You give me the idea yourself!
(GLENN *rises and leaves the pantry through the kitchen door. He appears in the living room, pauses for a mo-*

63

*ment, looking back, and then crosses and exits into
the den. Above,* ELEANOR *rises and leaves* RALPHIE'S
*room, leaving the door ajar. She crosses the hall and
enters the master bedroom, turns on the lights. She
gazes a moment at* DAN.

ELEANOR
(*Not quite a question*)

Dan . . .

DAN
(*Still sitting on the bed*)
I did what they told me. I saw the Wallings coming home
from the movies. I could've . . . (*Bursting out rebelliously*)
What *should* I have done, Ellie?

ELEANOR

Nothing. If the police come, Dan . . . it could be worse.

DAN

And if they don't? . . . You can't deal with boys like that.
With guns in their hands. Stone walls! If you could just *talk*
to them . . . *reason* . . . be sure he means what he . . .

ELEANOR

Dan . . . it won't be long now . . .

DAN
(*Rises*)
It makes no sense! You open a door . . . a door you've
opened thousands of times . . . and wham, all of a sudden
the whole world makes no sense!

ELEANOR
(*Moves to him, puts her hand on his shoulder*)
Dan, some day we'll look back on these hours and . . .

64

DAN

(Quietly)

Ellie, there is no *some day*. They've all been smashed now
. . . *(He sinks into chair)* broken off . . .

ELEANOR

They can't do this to you! I won't allow them to . . .

DAN

My brain's like a stone in my head. All this must've
started months ago . . . maybe years . . . when that kid
down there started hatching this scheme in his cell . . . before we ever even heard his name. . . .

ELEANOR

Dan, it's such a short, *short* time. Any minute now. All
they'll have is the car. Even that's insured . . . isn't it silly,
the things you think of? As soon as they've gone, you'll
pick up the phone . . .

(The expression on DAN's *face stops her. Across the
hall,* RALPHIE *rises from his bed and stands at his door,
listening.)*

DAN

(Turning away—flatly)

Just like that . . .

ELEANOR

(Sitting on bed, facing DAN)

Dan . . . what are you thinking?

DAN

I'm thinking a man could be haunted forever . . . after-
wards . . . by the thought that if he'd done just this at just
the right time . . . or that at just the proper moment . . .
he might have prevented it all.

ELEANOR

No, no, something else. When they leave you'll pick up the phone and . . . (*Stops; realizing*) They won't let you do that, will they?

DAN
(*Rising; speaks reassuringly now*)
Of course they will, darling. . . .

ELEANOR

No!

DAN

Shh . . .

ELEANOR

How can they stop it?

DAN

They can't. There's no way to . . .

ELEANOR
(*Finally*)
I know, Dan. I know.

DAN

Don't imagine things, Ellie!

ELEANOR
(*Hollowly*)
They'll have to take someone along. . . .

DAN
(*Turned away*)
No, Ellie, no. The thought never occurred to me. . . . I
. . I hope Cindy doesn't stay out too late, that's all.

ELEANOR

She won't take any chances, Dan.

66

DAN

(Turning, sees RALPHIE, *who has crossed into the room and stands at the door)*
Hey, skipper . . . what're you doing up this late?
(He knows RALPHIE *has heard, stops.* ELEANOR *rises and goes to* RALPHIE.*)*

RALPHIE

(To DAN, *their eyes locked)*
Are you going to let them . . . what you just said? . . .

DAN

Ralphie, I just explained to your mother . . .

ELEANOR

(Her arms around RALPHIE's *shoulders)*
Dear, your mother had a wild idea, that's all. Those men haven't even thought of that.

RALPHIE

I don't want them to take me along with them.

DAN

(Kneeling across the bed, takes RALPHIE's *shoulders)*
I wouldn't let them do that, Ralphie. You ought to *know* I wouldn't let them do that!

RALPHIE

(Backs away, turns and goes to the door)
How are you going to stop them?
*(*RALPHIE *turns away and goes to his door. He looks back at* DAN *and* ELEANOR, *then goes into his room and closes the door and sinks onto the bed.* DAN *and* ELEANOR *look at each other, helplessly. The sound of an approaching motorcar is heard. There is imme-*

diate tension. DAN *steps to the window. Below,* HANK *leaps to the side door, looks out the window, gun ready.*)

ELEANOR

Cindy?

DAN

Yes, dear . . . Cindy.
(ELEANOR *turns off the bedroom lights and she and* DAN *sit in the darkness on the bed. The car motor stops and two car doors slam. In pantry,* HANK *steps back from the side door. In the headlight beams from the car,* CINDY *appears outside, followed by* CHUCK, *who is a rather ordinary-appearing young man in his mid-twenties. He wears a sports coat and an expression of amazed bewilderment.*)

CHUCK

(*Catching up with her*)
Cindy . . . are you going in like this?

CINDY

(*At the step*)
Please, Chuck!

CHUCK

Look, I know I bowled you over. I've bowled myself over, too. But when a fellah proposes to a girl, he kind of expects an answer . . . like yes or no . . . not: "Take me home, Chuck!"

CINDY

(*Her mind elswhere*)
Was . . . was that a proposal?

68

CHUCK

Well, it wasn't much of one, but it was the best I could manage . . . with you off on another planet somewhere. I don't mind admitting you've got me so balled-up tonight, I . . . (*Shakes his head as* CINDY *fumbles in her pocket for her keys. He touches her arm*) Look . . : redhead . . .

CINDY

(*Whirling on him; sharply*)

Don't call me that!

CHUCK

But I always call you . . . All *right!* One minute you act like you hate me . . .

CINDY

Oh, no . . .

CHUCK

. . . and the next . . .

CINDY

Chuck . . .

CHUCK

(*Hopefully*)

Yes? . . .

CINDY

Chuck . . . listen.

CHUCK

Well? . . .

CINDY

(*Abruptly changing her mind*)

I'll tell you tomorrow . . . at the office.

CHUCK

You'll tell me one thing right now . . .

CINDY

(Tensely, turns away)
It doesn't concern you, Chuck.

CHUCK

(Turns her around, takes her hands)
If it concerns you, it concerns me. There. That's all I've
been trying to say all evening. You've done something to me,
Cindy. I've known a lot of girls . . . but . . . but you've
opened doors . . . in me . . . in the world. So I've got to know
. . . now . . . have I been kidding myself? Are you closing
the doors? *(Suddenly,* CINDY *throws her arms around his neck
and kisses him, in desperation, deeply touched, clinging to
him. He slips his arms around her waist. Inside,* HANK *is
watching . . . turns away. They break the kiss slowly and*
CINDY *lays her head against his chest)* Cindy . . . you're
trembling all over. *(He lifts her chin)* You'd better tell me.

CINDY

Yes . . .

CHUCK

Your family? . . . *(She nods)* Cindy, you can't fret about
it. If it's them. Because . . . look . . . it's *you. You're* the
one I want to take care of now. *Only* you. *(She stares, realizing that she cannot tell him)* Well, Cindy? *(*CINDY *shakes her
head. She turns to the door, taking out her keys.)*

CINDY

(With finality)
No! Good night, Chuck.

CHUCK

(Off on another tangent)
Your father doesn't like me. He thinks I've helled around
too much, maybe. . . .

70

CINDY

Please, Chuck . . .

CHUCK

Let's go in and talk it over with him. I . . .

CINDY

(*Turning on him—in desperation*)
Please . . . please . . . *please!*
(CHUCK, *with mingled disgust and defeat, takes the keys from her hand and unlocks the door.* HANK, *in the pantry, holds the automatic in readiness.* CINDY *pushes past* CHUCK *and blocks the door as he lets it swing open, the keys still in the lock.*)

CHUCK

All right, Cindy. I'm not coming in. . . .
(CINDY *closes the door in his face and leans limply against it, facing* HANK. CHUCK *stands for a moment staring at the door. Then, he turns away; suddenly he turns back and takes the keys from the lock and is about to call to* CINDY. *He thinks better of it, looks at the keys, then at the house, and turns and walks away, putting the keys in his pocket. There is the sound of one car door slam and the motor starts and the car drives away . . . the headlights dimming out quickly. Inside,* CINDY *moves toward the back stairs.*)

HANK

(*His voice sardonic, aping* GLENN's *manner*)
Use the other stairs, redhead. Glenn'll want to know you're home.
(CINDY *turns and leaves the pantry through the kitchen door. Above,* DAN *leaves the bedroom and goes to the head of the stairs. In the living room* ROBISH *turns on the lights. He is now quite drunk, his voice heavier*)

71

and louder than before. As CINDY *enters from the dining room, he leans across the stairs with his hand against the wall, blocking her way.)*

ROBISH

Have fun, sweetie? Parkin' with the boy friend. (HANK *appears in the dining-room door, the gun out of view)* He gettin' any, that guy?
(*Above,* DAN *turns on the light in the upstairs hall.* ELEANOR *comes to the door of the bedroom.)*

DAN

Cindy? . . .

HANK

(*Eyes on* ROBISH)
Get on upstairs, miss.
(DAN *descends the stairs and* ELEANOR *comes to the head of the stairs, leaning over the railing.)*

ROBISH

(*Voice blurred*)
Aw naw, aw naw. Ain't been searched yet. Got to search her first.

DAN

(*Taking in the situation swiftly . . . barks*)
Griffin!

ROBISH

Searched the ol' man, didn't we?

HANK

Get out of her way, Robish.
(GLENN *appears in the door of the den, immediately alert, throwing off sleep.)*

DAN

Griffin, if you intend to let him get away with this . . .

GLENN

(*Revolver in hand now*)
Stay where you are, Hilliard!

ROBISH

Pretty little gal might try to sneak a gun in. . . .

DAN

Griffin, you don't want to have to use that gun of yours,
do you?

GLENN

(*Grabs* ROBISH)
You goddam lunkhead . . .

ROBISH

(*With one swing of his arm throws* GLENN *back*)
Everybody givin' me orders! (*Steps toward* CINDY) Lift
your arms, baby.

DAN

(*Coming down between* ROBISH *and* CINDY)
A shot'll be heard, Griffin. . . .
(*But* HANK *steps in with the automatic drawn on*
ROBISH *and pushes* DAN *back onto the stairs. There is
a pause.* ROBISH *stands blinking owlishly at the auto-
matic.*)

GLENN

(*A breath*)
Hank . . . you damn fool.

ROBISH

(*Incredulously*)
Where'd ya get that?

73

HANK

(*Still covering* ROBISH)
You going up to bed now, miss?

ROBISH

(*Bawling*)
Where'd yuh get that gun?

GLENN

(*Shoves* ROBISH *toward dining room*)
Go sleep it off, Robish.

ROBISH

(*Turns at the dining room door*)
Turnin' on me, huh? All of yuh. (*Drunkenly maudlin*)
Turnin' on your ol' pal Robish. Okay. Ya wait. Ya-*all* wait.
. . .

(*He goes into the dining room. Above, for the first
time,* RALPHIE *moves: cautiously he opens the door of
his room.* ROBISH *appears in the pantry, staggering.*)

GLENN

What's it to you, Hank?

HANK

(*Muttering defensively*)
It ain't safe to touch the women.

GLENN

Yeah? . . .

CINDY

Thank you . . . Hank. . . .

HANK

(*After the briefest sort of pause*)
Get the hell to bed.

74

GLENN

(*Crosses toward* CINDY)

Don't get the idea you ain't gonna be searched, redhead!
(*At this point* ROBISH *goes out the side door, slamming it behind him. The significance of* ROBISH's *exit reaches* GLENN *in the living room. He springs into action.*)

GLENN

Christ! (*He runs through the dining-room door as he speaks*) Cover 'em, Hank. Let 'em have it if you have to!
(*He goes through the pantry and out the side door, slamming it as he goes.* DAN *turns to* CINDY; *then both turn to* HANK. *Gun pointed,* HANK *is tense all through . . . and uncertain.*)

HANK

Don't get the idea I won't . . .

ELEANOR

(*On stairs above*)

Dan?

DAN

Stay up there, Ellie . . . hear?

HANK

(*A warning*)

Don't get any ideas now. . . .

DAN

(*To* CINDY)

Cindy! You look . . . (*He glances at* HANK, *then back to* CINDY) Are you sick?

CINDY

No, I . . .

> (CINDY *turns to* DAN. *Their eyes meet. Pause. And then*
> CINDY *collapses.* DAN *takes a step toward her. She*
> *holds onto the back of the chair and sinks into it.*)

ELEANOR

Cindy!

HANK

Don't move, mister!

DAN

Dammit, this child's sick. If there's any decency in you at
all . . .

> (RALPHIE *appears in the pantry, coming down the back*
> *stairs. He listens a moment, then goes to the side door*
> *and opens it.*)

HANK

If you're trying to . . . (RALPHIE *slams the side door as he*
goes out into the darkness) Glenn? . . . (*There is no reply.*
HANK, *utterly bewildered, motions* DAN *into the corner and*
moves cautiously to CINDY) She's just scared, I guess. . . .
(*He bends over* CINDY) Miss . . . no need to be . . .

> (CINDY *moves with animal swiftness. She grasps*
> HANK's *arm and sinks her teeth into his wrist, hard.*
> HANK *drops the automatic on the floor in front of*
> CINDY. *He utters a cry of pain and surprise and*
> *straightens up, holding his wrist.* DAN *moves in with*
> *his right arm encircling* HANK's *shoulders, pinning his*
> *hands to his chest.* CINDY *picks up the automatic and*
> *stands ready.* DAN *drags* HANK *to the front door and*
> *opens it.* HANK *calls for* "Glenn," *but* DAN *succeeds in*
> *pushing him out the door.* DAN *closes and locks the*
> *door as* CINDY *runs across the room to the light switch.*
> *She turns off the living-room lights. There is only the*
> *light flooding down the stairs from the upstairs hall.*)

DAN

Ellie! Get on the phone up there! (CINDY *crosses to hand* DAN *the automatic*) Cindy . . . lock the back door!
> (*Above,* ELEANOR *goes down the hall and notices the door to* RALPHIE'S *room open. She steps in and calls. Then she goes into the master bedroom and calls.*)

ELEANOR

Ralphie! . . . Ralphie!
> (CINDY *goes through the dining room on the run and into the pantry, where she locks the side door and returns to the living room.*)

DAN

Ellie, for God's sake, get on the phone! Stay away from the windows, hear!
> (*He impatiently picks up the phone and dials the operator.*)

ELEANOR
> (*In master bedroom*)

Dan!
> (*She runs to the head of the stairs.*)

DAN

Operator. *Operator!*
> (CINDY *returns to the living room and starts up the front stairs.*)

ELEANOR

Don't, Dan . . . for God's sake! (*Screams*) Dan, don't! *Ralphie's not in the house!*
> (CINDY *freezes on the stairs, looks at* DAN. DAN *stands with the phone in his hand.*)

77

OPERATOR

(*On phone*)

Operator. Operator. This is your operator. Your call, please? Your call, please? . . .

(DAN *replaces the phone.*)

DAN

(*A whisper*)

God Almighty.

CINDY

Maybe he got away.

(*Another pause, shorter; then* GLENN *appears outside at the side door with* RALPHIE. GLENN *has* RALPHIE'S *arm pinned behind him and holds the boy as a shield. They move to the steps, out of sight of the door.*)

GLENN

Hilliard! Can you hear me in there, Hilliard?

RALPHIE

(*Plaintively*)

Dad! Dad, he's hurting my arm.

ELEANOR

(*In terror*)

Dan, was that Ralphie? *Was that Ralphie?*

DAN

Stay up there, Ellie! (*Calling slightly louder*) Don't shout out there, Griffin! (*Then, lower*) Cindy, take your mother to her room. If you hear a shot . . . make the call!

(DAN *goes through the dining-room door and on into the pantry.* CINDY *goes up the front stairs.* ELEANOR *goes into the master bedroom and stands near the door.* CINDY *picks up the extension phone in the up-*

78

stairs hall, but keeps her hand on the circuit breaker. She is tense, waiting, her attention turned toward the stairs. DAN *is in the pantry.*)

GLENN

(*A loud whisper*)

We go now, Hilliard . . . they find the brat in a ditch. (DAN *unlocks and opens the side door*) Turn on the light. And toss out the automatic.

DAN

Let the boy come in, Griffin.

GLENN

Lights first. Then the gun. (DAN *turns on the pantry light. Then he tosses the automatic out.* GLENN *pushes* RALPHIE *up the steps and into the pantry before him*) You're both covered, Pop.

RALPHIE

(*Still defiant*)

I . . . I tried.

DAN

(*Gently*)

So did I. Go up to your mother now.

(RALPHIE *slips behind the open door and mounts the rear stairs.* HANK *appears outside and picks up the automatic.*)

GLENN

(*Casually, to* HANK)

Get the lunkhead inside.

(GLENN *faces* DAN.)

HANK

(*Off*)

On your feet, Robish.

79

GLENN

Couldn't wait, could you, Pop? Less'n a hour an' you couldn't wait.

(HANK *appears, the gun in hand, urging a staggering* ROBISH, *who is groggy, holding his head.* HANK *guides him through the pantry and into the living room.*)

ROBISH

(*As he passes through the pantry*)
Wha' happened? What . . .

HANK

Shut up!

(ROBISH *and* HANK *appear in the living room.* ROBISH *flops on the sofa.* HANK *stands at the foot of the stairs.* GLENN *closes the side door.*)

GLENN

I hadda put Robish on ice for a while, Pop . . . cause he couldn't learn who was runnin' things aroun' here. I guess I gotta learn you, too.

(GLENN *strikes* DAN's *left shoulder with his left fist, violently. Then* GLENN *strikes him a stomach blow with the pistol in his right hand.* DAN *crumples and falls.* GLENN *kneels over him and strikes three violent blows with the pistol.* DAN *doesn't move. All this is very silent.* GLENN *rises, turns and locks the side door . . . and steps over* DAN's *body, goes through the kitchen door and into the living room through the dining-room door.* HANK *follows him with his eyes as* GLENN *crosses slowly to sit in the chair at the window. He looks up at* HANK. *Their eyes meet.* HANK *sits slowly on the stairs. The lights begin to dim slowly.*)

Very slow curtain

ACT TWO

ACT TWO

Outside the window, night. The clock reads 12:04. CARSON, *seated at desk, plays solitaire.* WINSTON *sits curled up awkwardly on chair.* BARD *leans against files, thumbing through telephone-reports. A long pause.* CARSON *glances at his watch.*

CARSON

It's another day . . . in case anyone's interested.

BARD

There's a full moon, too. So what? (*Holding up the reports*) Collect calls . . . person-to-person . . . pay stations. Would you believe this many people sit up talking on the telephone at night? Why the hell don't they go to bed?
(*Drops the reports on the desk.*)

WINSTON

Why don't we?

CARSON

(*Picking up the reports*)
You've got all the reasons right here. . . . Sickness . . . impulse . . . birth . . . death . . . drunkenness . . . love . . . hate . . .

BARD

What the hell're you . . . a poet or something?

CARSON

It'll break, Bard. You can stretch a wire just so tight.

83

DUTCH'S VOICE
(*On intercom*)

Jess . . . that 11:02 person-to-person from Columbus to Blackstone 2726 . . .

BARD
(*Flipping intercom button*)

Yeah, yeah?

DUTCH'S VOICE

It was the daughter calling to say the honeymoon was already a huge success.

BARD

Great!

DUTCH'S VOICE

My theory is this Helen Laski found another guy and climbed in the hay.

(BARD *flips off the intercom.* WINSTON *rises sleepily.*)

WINSTON

I'll be in the file room, flat on my face. *My* theory is this Helen Laski don't believe in telephones. Uses carrier pigeons. Has a secret compartment in her brassière.

(WINSTON *exits. Outside, a police siren is heard fading in and coming to a stop.*)

CARSON
(*Shuffling cards*)

You'd find double solitaire kind of restful.

BARD

Carson, you deal me just one of those cards and I'm gonna report you to J. Edgar Hoover. (*Shaking head but smiling faintly*) Isn't it just my luck to meet up with a character like you on a night like this?

CARSON

You're not such hot company yourself. . . . Ten bucks says they're in Denver . . . or New Orleans . . . or Nome, Alaska, by now.

BARD

They're here.

CARSON

Who told you . . . that monkey on your back?

BARD

I say they're here, Carson, because Glenn Griffin's got all kinds of dark pockets in his mind . . . all kinds of weird twists. (*Pacing*) He's always acting, for one thing . . . trying to live up to some phony picture he carries around in that snarled-up brain of his . . . some stupid, childish image of what a really clever criminal should be.

CARSON
(*Shrugs*)

Well, that's a good reason. It doesn't explain why he's in town, but it's a good reason. Any others?

BARD
(*Sits*)

Carson, did you ever look into the eyes of one of those crazy kids . . . and hear him say, "You got yours coming, copper"? Between his teeth . . . with his broken jaw wired up tight . . . "I'll get you." *That's* why I know he's here and that's why *I'm* going to get to him before he gets to *me*. (*Rises*) Any objections, Carson?

CARSON

No objections, Bard. But if we catch up with him . . . our job's to arrest, if possible.

85

THE DESPERATE HOURS

BARD
You remindin' me who's actually in charge here, Carson?

CARSON
Something like that. My friends call me Harry.
(*He goes back to his cards.*)

BARD
Well, I'll tell you right now . . . I'm making no promises
. . . Harry.

(*Dimout*)

HILLIARD HOME

Dimness over all the house. GLENN *is at the living-
room window, smoking. The window curtains are
parted slightly.* HANK *is in the pantry, sitting on the
back stairs.* CINDY *sits in* RALPHIE's *bedroom.* RALPHIE
is on the bed asleep. In the master bedroom, DAN *is
stretched out on the bed with a damp towel folded and
placed over his forehead.* ELEANOR *sits on the twin bed,
facing him, with a dry towel in her hands.*

ELEANOR
(*Softly*)
Darling . . . can you hear me? I want you to promise . . .

DAN
What? Oh . . . I must've dozed off. Isn't that . . . remark-
able?

ELEANOR
You needed it. I slipped off myself several times . . . but
I heard every sound . . . every car that went by.
(DAN *stirs.*)

86

DAN

What time is it?

(ELEANOR *reaches out and turns on the lamp on the night table between the beds. She looks at the clock on the table.*)

ELEANOR

After one . . .

DAN

(*Trying to sit up*)

Midnight. He said mid . . .

ELEANOR

Shhh. Don't move. Listen. What you did—what you tried —that was a foolish and terrible and wonderful thing . . . (*Shakes her head as though trying to clear it*) No, no, that's not what I meant to say. Dan, you must never do anything like that again. Ever. You . . . you might have been killed. I want you to promise me now. Dan, are you listening?

DAN

What're they doing down there? Why haven't they gone?

ELEANOR

Dan, please. Nobody knows anything about what's happening here. Nobody in the world. We're all alone in this. Dan, I'm pleading with you. . . .

DAN

Ellie . . . how long has it been since I said I love you?

ELEANOR

Dan . . .

DAN

Why shouldn't a man say it? Why didn't I say it all the time . . . over and over?

ELEANOR

You didn't need . . .

DAN

Ellie, why'm I so grouchy in the mornings? No, that's not what I mean . . . I mean . . . what's the matter, people don't laugh more? Waking up . . . seeing the sun . . . That . . . that was a funny joke Ralphie told . . . about the moron and the icebox.

ELEANOR
(Smiling wanly)

Not very . . .

DAN

All right, it was lousy. Is that any reason not to laugh? (*In awe*) God . . . this morning. How many hours ago? It's . . . it's like looking back on something that happened . . . a whole lifetime ago. (*Reaches out his right hand to her face*) Your face . . . darling, you're beautiful. Do you know that? I must've been deaf, dumb and blind. For years.

ELEANOR
(Takes his hand in hers)

Dan . . . you haven't promised.
(DAN *sits up with difficulty.*)

DAN

Ellie . . . I can't. I'm feeling along a blank wall. In the dark. If I find a hole . . . or even a crack . . . I've got to explore it. There's light behind that wall, Ellie. I never knew how much. There was light there once and there's got to be light again!

THE DESPERATE HOURS

ELEANOR

Dan, look at yourself. Your head. Next time . . . you don't know. *You don't know.* He'll kill you.

DAN

(Grimly)

He won't kill me as long as he needs me. *(Suddenly)* You look so *tired.* Damn them! *(Gently)* When this is over, we're going to have a maid here. A full-time maid.

ELEANOR

You wouldn't really like it, Dan. None of us like having strangers in the . . .
  (She breaks off, realizing what she is saying. Their eyes meet. Pause. Then, there is the sound of a branch cracking off a tree and brushing down the side of the house. She starts and crumples. DAN *holds her. Below,* GLENN *looks out the living-room window.* HANK *rises and looks out the window in the side door.)*

DAN

It's all right, dear. It's all right. Only one of those dead branches off the oak. *(He takes her into his arms)* My God, Ellie . . . it's a jungle. We jump at nothing. That's how you slept, isn't it . . . like an animal in the . . .
  (The telephone rings, cutting him off. In the living room, GLENN *quickly steps to the phone and turns on the hall light.* HANK *runs up the back stairs to the extension phone in the upstairs hall.* CINDY *rises and opens the door of* RALPHIE'S *room.* RALPHIE *doesn't stir.* DAN *opens the bedroom door.)*

GLENN

I'll take it, Hank.

89

HANK

(*Ready at the phone upstairs*)

I'm here, Glenn.

(HANK *takes up the phone after* GLENN *answers and stands staring at* CINDY *in the door of* RALPHIE'S *room as he listens.*)

GLENN

(*Picks up the phone downstairs*)

Hello? . . . Put her on. . . . Yeah, this is Mr. James. *Put her on!* . . . Hi, doll, what's up? . . . Where are you? . . . Mmm— okay, get this. That stuff you're carrying . . . put it in a en- velope . . . an' take down this address . . . Daniel C. Hil- liard . . .

(GLENN *continues, but his voice is* under *the following dialogue so that the address is not heard.*)

HANK

(*To* CINDY, *harshly*)

Stay inside an' shut the door, redhead.

(CINDY, *in defiance, doesn't move.*)

ELEANOR

Dan, what is it?

DAN

Shhh . . .

GLENN

(*Under above dialogue*)

. . . 243 North Central Avenue. . . . Soon's I get it, we'll make tracks, doll. . . . See you Louisville. You know where.

(GLENN *hangs up.* HANK *replaces the extension phone and comes down the front stairs and is about to go into the dining room. He stops in door when* DAN *comes downstairs.* DAN *follows* HANK *down the hall and comes near the bottom of the stairs.*)

ELEANOR
(*Follows* DAN *to the bedroom door*)
Dan!

DAN
(*As he comes down the stairs*)
Griffin! Who was that? What's happening?

GLENN
(*Casually*)
Tell you in the morning, Pop . . . after breakfast.

DAN
(*Shocked*)
After break— You'll tell me now!

GLENN
(*Angry*)
What's another day, Pop? Get some shuteye. You're gonna need it.
(GLENN *turns his back on* DAN *and walks toward the window.* DAN *starts toward* GLENN.)

HANK
Glenn! Watch it!
(GLENN *whirls.* DAN *stops, looks at* HANK, *then at* GLENN, *and turns and goes up the stairs.* ELEANOR *moves into bedroom and stands waiting for* DAN. CINDY, *who has been waiting at the head of the stairs, goes into her room and closes the door.* GLENN *goes to the window, picks up the road map from the table, and stands in the window, studying it.* HANK *goes into the pantry and stands looking out the window of the side door.*)

ELEANOR
(*As* DAN *comes into the bedroom*)
Well? . . .

91

DAN
(*Flatly . . . low*)
They're not going.

ELEANOR

Oh Dan, no!

DAN
(*Suddenly the violence in him mounts to a determined grim-ness*)
They're going!
(DAN *turns to the door.* ELEANOR *stops him. The following builds in intensity until they are almost snarling at each other.*)

ELEANOR

Dan, you promised, you promised!

DAN
(*Erupting slightly*)
Ellie, don't tie my hands! I'm tied up enough already!

ELEANOR
(*Desperately*)
If you go down there now, something terrible is going to happen. I know it. I *feel* it.

DAN

How long can we go on sitting on top of a volcano?

ELEANOR
(*Takes his hand, tugging at him*)
Dan, you're going to lie down now! I'm telling you!

DAN
(*Shouting, throws her off*)
You're not telling me what to do! (*Pause. They are appalled. They stand looking at each other for a moment. Then*

they go into each other's arms. DAN *says, almost whispering*)
Ellie, what're we doing? What're we *doing?* (*Slight pause*)
How can he know, that scum down there . . . how can he
know how to do this? A boy who never loved anyone in his
life.

> (ELEANOR *turns out the bed lamp and sits on the bed.*
> DAN *sits beside her and puts his arms around her. Be-*
> *low,* GLENN *flicks the map with his fingers and exits;*
> *goes into the pantry.* HANK *turns away from the door.*)

HANK

Glenn . . . we gotta get outta here. What if they trace that
call?

GLENN
(*Grinning*)
You ever hear of a burg called Circleville, Ohio? It's nineteen miles south-a Columbus. Them dumb coppers might
be tracin' calls outta Columbus, Hank, but not outta no jerk-
town like Circleville.

HANK
(*Turns back to the window*)
We'd be better off anywhere but here.

GLENN

It can't be nowhere else but here. With that much dough
. . . in this town . . . I can have that copper put on ice for
good.

HANK
(*Shaking his head*)
That one idea . . .

GLENN

Yeah, that one idea. Kid, you gotta stick with me on this.
You're . . . Hank, you're all I got. You know that. It's you'n
me against 'em all!

HANK

(*Trapped: conflicting emotions. He turns to the window*)
I know, I know . . .
    (GLENN *grabs him, turns him around.*)

GLENN

You know . . . you know! You don't know nothin'! I gotta
get this outta my brain. I gotta sleep again. You didn't lay in
that bed . . . pain twistin' down in your gut . . ̇. months . . .
jaw clamped up in a vise . . . eatin' that slop through a tube
. . . *months* . . . till pretty soon there ain't nothin' in your
mind but the face-a the guy that done it. Me with my hands
up . . . tossin' out my gun . . . and that bastard walkin' up'n
cloutin' me. I can still hear the way the bone cracked. . . .
An' me with my hands up!

(*Blackout*)

SHERIFF'S OFFICE
    Clock: 6:15. Early morning. CARSON *is seated.* BARD
is rising from behind the desk.

BARD

Yeah, he had his hands up. Trying to surrender. *After* he'd
plugged one of the best damn cops ever walked. While
Jerry was laying there twisting and screaming in the gutter
. . . with a bullet in a nerve . . . *then* Griffin throws out his
empty gun and steps out of the doorway of that hotel, big as
life. Only I didn't let him get away with it. I let him have it.
One crack . . . right in that grinning face of his. (*Rubbing
his fist*) If I'd only arrested him . . . or shot him before he
gave up . . . he'd probably've forgotten it. But according to
his warped code, *I* double-crossed *him.*

94

CARSON
(*Quietly*)
Under the circumstances . . . police code, too.

BARD
(*Leans over desk*)
Listen! That kid's as ruthless as they come! He'd as soon kill a human being as step on a bug.

CARSON
All right . . . so civilization didn't take. In his case. But we've climbed a long way out of the slime, Jess. Maybe that slime still clings to some of us. *Them.* But you're a police officer, Jess . . . and civilized men can't let the slime on *them* drag *us* back down. If we don't live by the rules, the rules will soon disappear. Then . . . (*Shrugs*) we're all right back where we started.

BARD
Rules! He was sentenced to ten years. He'd have been out again anyway inside of three more.

CARSON
Which only proves it's a pretty ramshackle system. But it's all we've got. You had no right to break his jaw. And if we find him, you've no right to kill him unless it's the only way to stop him.

BARD
(*Sits on edge of desk; bitterly*)
Sure, send him back to that cardboard prison . . . so he can start all over again.

CARSON
No choice, Jess. Unless you want to become just like him. In that case, he wins, anyway. (*Rises*) I'm ready for breakfast. How about you?
(BARD, *thoughtful for a moment, looks at* CARSON, *rises.*)

95

BARD

Yeah.

(*Dimout*)

HILLIARD HOME

It is morning. ELEANOR *is seated on the sofa,*
RALPHIE *beside her.* HANK *stands at the window, smok-*
ing. DAN *is entering from the dining room, followed by*
GLENN. GLENN *picks his teeth with finger and wipes*
hand on sofa.)

GLENN

Lady, that 'as a goddam good breakfast. (*Takes* HANK's
cigarette, turns to DAN) Hilliard, you ever broke, your woman
can support you good. Cookin'.
  (*Takes a drag on the cigarette and returns it to* HANK.)

DAN
(*Sitting in chair*)
How much longer, Griffin?

GLENN

Hell, you don't have any worse headache'n Robish 'n
there ... (*Gestures into the den*) and he's nursin' a hangover
to boot.

DAN
(*Level and insistent*)
How long?

GLENN

Till I get a certain envelope in the mail. Meantime ...
everything goes on just like before aroun' here. You'n the
redhead go to work.

HANK

Glenn, if he's gonna be gone all day outta the house ...

96

GLENN

You don't trust Hilliard, Hank? Now me—I trust the old gink. You know why? I got him where the hair's short, that's why. Junior here gets a break. He misses a day of school. (CINDY *comes out of her room and down the stairs*) Won't hurt you none, kid. Missed a few myself.

CINDY
(*At foot of stairs; scornfully*)
And look at you.

RALPHIE
(*Kneeling on sofa*)
I'd just as soon go. . . .

GLENN
(*Crosses to* CINDY)
Yeah, you're lookin', Sis. Pass you on the street, you'd look right through us both. You're seein' us now, redhead.

CINDY

No comment.

GLENN
(*To* DAN)
Now, get the lead outta your . . . (*The thud of the newspaper is heard against the front door. The* HILLIARDS *are not startled but* GLENN *and* HANK *jump into action.* HANK, *drawing the automatic, moves up to the door.* GLENN, *with the .38 ready, covers the family.* HANK *unlocks and opens the door a crack. He kneels down and reaches out with his left hand to bring in the paper.* HANK *rises, closing the door, and hands the paper to* GLENN. GLENN *unfolds the paper.* HANK *locks the door.* RALPHIE, *who has been watching it all, snickers. After a split-second pause*) Get your kicks young, kid. (*To* DAN) You don't want to be late for that time-clock, Pop.

(ELEANOR *rises and crosses to* GLENN, *fire in her eyes.*)

97

ELEANOR

Why do you want to go on torturing my husband? You know what he'll be thinking . . . wondering . . . imagining . . . in that office! You take pleasure in torturing him, don't you?

GLENN

(Easily)

Lady, I take pleasure in looking out for my own skin . . . and Hank's.

DAN

(In warning)

Ellie . . .

ELEANOR

No, no, it's some sort of cruel, inhuman, sadistic game with you. You're playing a *game!*

(Abruptly, she explodes into violence; slaps GLENN *full across the face.* DAN *steps in, grabs her and swings her around to the far end of the sofa, then turns to look at* GLENN. *The family is in a small group, defiant. Long pause, while* GLENN *rubs his jaw.)*

GLENN

(Quietly, sitting)

Whole family gettin' tough this morning. Nothin' personal, ma'am.

DAN

(Grimly—knowing)

It's personal all right. In some strange mixed-up way.

GLENN

Clickety-click. Don't get ulcers tryin' to dope it, Pop. (*To* CINDY) You, redhead. Keep that pretty mouth shut today, see.

Or that boy friend of yours ain't gonna want to take you on no more rides. Not after Robish gets done with you.
(*Pause.*)

DAN
(*Deciding—a step*)
I'm not leaving this house today.

GLENN
(*Hardening*)
You ain't learned yet who's runnin' it?

HANK
(*Steps near* GLENN)
Glenn, I think . . .

GLENN
(*Rising; exploding*)
You think! With what? I'm lookin' out for you, you slobberin' pukin' little bastard. Now get in there and turn on the news reports! (GLENN *turns to* DAN) You ain't had nothin', Pop. Nothin' like what you deserve.

DAN
Deserve? . . .

GLENN
Yeah . . . deserve! You'n your fancy carpet and your big lawn'n your goddam snazzy car!

DAN
(*Takes a step toward* GLENN)
Griffin . . . (ELEANOR *touches* DAN's *arm to restrain him but he pulls away and continues*) you're not going to take it out on me and my family because you hate the world! I've worked for every cent I ever made . . . worked hard . . . for this house, that car . . . and I'm proud of it. That table you've

99

scarred with your whisky . . . the furniture you've wiped your
filthy hands on . . . the carpet you've burnt holes in. Proud
because I *did* work for it!

GLENN

(*Spits on carpet with contempt*)
Sucker! Just like our old man, ain't he, Hank?

DAN

I pity the poor man!

GLENN

Don't waste your time. He kicked off while we was in re-
form school. He was a *proud* bastard, too. Now get outta
here!

DAN

I'm staying right here!

GLENN

(*Violent*)
Hilliard, I told you . . . (*Changes—shrugs*) Okay . . . (*Sits*)
Okay . . . You stay . . . an' we stay. 'Cause we ain't gonna beat
it outta here till we get that dough. An' that dough's in a
letter . . . addressed to you . . . at your office. (*Pause. The fight
goes out of* DAN) We don't want no Federal men tracin' anything up to your front door here, do we? . . . See, Pop, I'm
thinkin' of you.

(ELEANOR *takes* DAN'S *arm.*)

ELEANOR

He'll go. He's going. (*As* CINDY *moves to closet and gets
her own coat and brings* DAN'S *coat to him*) Dan, I'll be upstairs with Ralphie. If one of them starts up the stairs, I'll
scream so loud they'll *have* to use their guns. That'll be the
end of it. For them too. Now I'll get your coat. It's getting
colder every minute. . . .

(CINDY *already stands waiting with* DAN'S *coat.*)

DAN

I . . . I can hold my own coat, Cindy.

CINDY

Maybe I'd *like* to hold your coat.
(DAN *climbs into coat, then turns to* ELEANOR.)

ELEANOR

Careful now, Dan . . . I know, I say that every morning of the world, don't I?
(DAN *takes* ELEANOR *in his arms. They kiss . . . with great meaning and tenderness, in sharp contrast to yesterday morning's casual good-bye.* GLENN *makes a kissing sound with his mouth, then makes a pop with his finger in his mouth.* HANK *takes a step down as* GLENN *laughs mockingly.*)

HANK

What's so funny? (*As* GLENN *frowns, the laughter dying*) I don't see nothin' so funny, you should break your neck laughin'.

GLENN

I laugh when I feel like it. You don't have a goddam thing to say about it. That right? . . . That right, Hank?

HANK

I never had nothin' to say about anything.
(HANK *turns on his heel and goes through the dining-room door and into the pantry.* CINDY *steps down to* RALPHIE, *and tousles his hair.*)

CINDY
(*Softly*)

Mister pest to you.

GLENN

You, Hilliard. That nick on your head—you got a story ready? 'Cause it wouldn't take much of a slip today, Pop. Just a little one and . . . you're gonna wish you never come back through that door.

DAN

(Quietly . . . with dignity and force)

Griffin . . . you're staying here now for only one reason. To get a man killed. A man who did something to you. I couldn't understand that before. Now I can. I understand it because I'm more like you now than you know. If any harm comes to anyone in this house, Griffin, I'm going to kill you. Me. No matter what it takes . . . whether the police capture you first or not . . . if it takes my whole life, Griffin, I'll find you and I'll kill you. Do you understand that?

GLENN

(Impressed but attempting swagger)

Pop . . . you're a regular comedian.

DAN

Do you understand that?

GLENN

Sure, Pop . . . I got you. All the way.

DAN

And if not you, Griffin . . . your brother.

GLENN

(Immediately tense, violent; leaps up)

You come near Hank and . . .

DAN

(Firmly)

That's the deal, Griffin. That's the deal. You've turned me into your kind of animal now.

102

(GLENN *does not move.* DAN *turns, takes a long look at*
RALPHIE, *then* ELEANOR. CINDY *opens the door.* DAN
follows CINDY *out, closing the door behind him.*)

GLENN

(*Moving up to the door*)

Lady . . . you didn't know what a tough old bird you married, did you?

ELEANOR

(*Softly*)

No. No, I didn't.
(*She sits quietly.*)

GLENN

(*Calls*)

Robish! (*As* GLENN *moves into the dining room,* ROBISH
*enters from the den and sits. He is suffering from a hangover
and from last night's violence.* GLENN *appears in the pantry.*
HANK *is now standing at the window of the side door, watching* DAN *and* CINDY *drive away.* GLENN *stands for a moment,
looks down at the radio, bends down and turns it on. Music
rises*) You ain't interested in the news?

HANK

Same old stuff. That car. That's all they got. (*Faces* GLENN
suddenly) Glenn . . . why're you crowdin' it? Why go on
takin' these chances?

GLENN

You don't take chances, you might as well be dead.
(*The sound of an old truck approaching fades in.*)

HANK

That's what we're gonna be . . . all of us . . . this keeps up.

103

GLENN

You start yammerin' again, I'm gonna give you a belt across the . . . (*They hear the truck. Immediate tension.* GLENN *tries to see out the window of the side door, then rushes into the living room.* ELEANOR *has risen and crossed up to the window.* HANK *stays looking out the window of the side door*) Who is it, lady?

ELEANOR

Only Mr. Patterson. He . . . he hauls away the trash.

GLENN

Okay, let him get it and clear out.

ELEANOR

Only . . . he'll . . . this is the end of the month. He'll come to the door to collect.

GLENN
(*Calls*)

Hank! (HANK *leaves the pantry and comes into living room*) Okay, pay him. (ELEANOR *goes to pick up her checkbook from sofa.* GLENN *turns to* RALPHIE) Upstairs, kid. And not a squeak. (RALPHIE, *on sofa, folds arms, doesn't move*) Take him up, Hank, and keep his mouth shut.
  (HANK *lifts* RALPHIE *off the sofa, sets him on his feet and pushes him upstairs.* ELEANOR *goes into the pantry.* MR. PATTERSON *appears outside and knocks at the side door. Above,* HANK *stands at the door of* RALPHIE'S *room, listening.* RALPHIE *sits on the bed.*)

ROBISH
(*Miserable*)

My gut's growling.

GLENN

Knock off.

104

ROBISH

Jeez, I forgot what a headache feels like. . . .

GLENN

Shut up!
> (ELEANOR *opens the side door and admits* MR. PATTER-SON *to the pantry.*)

ELEANOR

Just a minute. Mr. Patterson, while I . . . You stay here, please. . . .

PATTERSON
> (*Pushes right in*)

Don't mind if I do. . . . (ELEANOR *returns to the living room*) Wind always puts a nasty nip in the air . . . raises merry . . . (*He sees that* ELEANOR *has gone, raises his voice*) raises merry cain with my arthritis.
> (PATTERSON, *through the following, notices with in-terest the small radio, the stacked cigarette butts, the chair. He gathers up the newspapers and places them on the chair, glancing with some interest at the head-lines. In the living room* ELEANOR *sits on the sofa and writes the check on the coffee table.* GLENN *leans over the back of the sofa, watching her.*)

GLENN
> (*Whisper*)

You always pay the old gink with a check?

ROBISH

Who the hell is it?
> (GLENN *silences* ROBISH *with a gesture.*)

ELEANOR

Yes, yes, my husband . . . (*Then firmly*) my husband thinks it's not safe to have cash in the house. (*Signs*) That's *funny*, isn't it?

PATTERSON

You speaking to me, Mrs. Hilliard?

ELEANOR
(*Rises*)

No, Mr. Patterson, I'm coming.
(GLENN *stops* ELEANOR, *takes the check and examines it.*)

GLENN

Hank's upstairs with the brat. Be careful.
(*He returns the check to* ELEANOR, *who goes into the pantry.*)

ROBISH
(*Rises*)

Who is that out . . .

GLENN
(*At dining-room door, listening*)

Shut up!
(ROBISH *and* GLENN *listen,* GLENN *holding the dining-room door slightly open.*)

PATTERSON
(*As* ELEANOR *enters the pantry*)

You . . . uh . . . got company, Mrs. Hilliard?

ELEANOR

Company?

PATTERSON

Well . . . I notice things, y'know. Always have. (*Takes the check from* ELEANOR'S *hand*) Thank you, thank you! (*Peering*) You feelin' yourself, Mrs. Hilliard?

ELEANOR

(Desperate to get him out)

Only . . . I've got a slight cold. Nothing . . .

PATTERSON

(Turns and opens the door)

We-ell, lotta colds around. Flu, too. Bad year for the flu, y'know. *(In the doorway, he turns back)* Your daughter buy herself another one of them second-hand cars?

ELEANOR

(Holding the door open for him)

No. No!

(In panic, she closes the door in his face, leans against it. GLENN *rushes into the pantry, followed by* ROBISH. HANK *looks out the window of* RALPHIE'S *room.* PATTERSON, *after a look back at the house, disappears.* GLENN *pushes* ELEANOR *upstage and looks out the window of the side door.)*

ROBISH

He's snoopin' around the garage.

ELEANOR

Oh, no, he's only taking the trash from the containers alongside.

ROBISH

Up on his toes lookin' in the windows!

ELEANOR

On Thursday mornings he always . . .

HANK

(Leaving RALPHIE'S *room to run down back stairs)*

Glenn! He wrote something down.

ROBISH

Griffin, that joker wrote down the license. I seen him! Fork over the gun.

ELEANOR

I'm sure he . . .

GLENN

(Locked in indecision)
Dry up, both-a-you, I'm thinkin'.

ROBISH

He's climbin' in the cab of the truck. *Gimme the gun!* I can hop on the back.

HANK

(At foot of back stairs)
Glenn . . . we don't want a murder rap ridin' us!
(GLENN meets HANK's eyes, then, with a smile of defiance and revenge, hands the gun to ROBISH. The truck door is heard being slammed. Then, the motor starting and failing . . . starting and failing under the following.)

GLENN

(To ROBISH)
You call me on the phone. An' stay outta sight till it's dark, see. I'll have Hilliard bring you back. Use your head for a change!

ROBISH

(Going out the side door on the run)
My head feels better already.
(As ROBISH disappears, the truck motor catches and we hear it start up, shift, and drive away. HANK looks pale and sick. ELEANOR, stunned, moves dazedly toward the living room.)

ELEANOR

He . . . he knew nothing. (*Corrects self*) Knows nothing.
(*She goes into the living room and sinks onto the sofa
slowly, beginning to weep.*)

HANK

Glenn, are you crazy? Hilliard won't bring Robish back in
here.

GLENN

He will when I'm done with him on the phone. Pop don't
want Robish picked up any more'n we do . . . an' tippin' the
cops this address. (*Suddenly grabs* HANK, *pushes him against
wall of the pantry*) What's the matter with you anyway, kid?
You got a weak stomach after all? (HANK *turns his head away*)
What're you stewin' about? You're free, ain't you?

HANK

(*Wrenches himself loose, starts for kitchen door*)
I was free-er in that cell!
(HANK *goes into the living room. After a second* GLENN
follows him. HANK *ignores* GLENN *and goes to the den
door with a side glance at* ELEANOR; *he slams the
door.* GLENN *is baffled and angry.*)

GLENN

(*To* ELEANOR)
Lady! Shut up that wailin'! Go some place else'n cry!
(ELEANOR *rises slowly and, with difficulty, mounts the
stairs.*)

ELEANOR

Poor man . . . that poor old man . . . he wouldn't hurt a fly.

(*Dimout*)

SHERIFF'S OFFICE

Darkness outside. WINSTON *is seated,* BARD *is pacing.*

BARD

Who'd want to pump three slugs in the back of an innocent old guy like that?

WINSTON

Who can say? Somebody settling an old score . . . old
crony he cheated at cards. . . .

BARD

Sixty-three years old, half-crippled with arthritis . . .
wouldn't harm a fly. (BARD *looks up as* FREDERICKS *enters.*
LT. FREDERICKS *is an older man, crisp and efficient, with a
weathered face. He wears a State Police uniform*) Fredericks, are we going to get that stuff from the state's attorney's
office or aren't we?

FREDERICKS

Carson's prying it out of them. Bard, why make so much
of an old garbage man gettin' bumped?

BARD

He was killed by a .38. The prison guard at Terre Haute . . .

FREDERICKS

Sure, there's only one .38 in the state! Deputy, you got a
obsession. You can't tie in every crime in the area with those
three.

BARD

I reckon not, Lieutenant. Only *you* tell *me* why anybody'd
. . . (*Breaks off as* CARSON *enters*) Well, Carson?

110

CARSON

(Tearing the top off large manila envelope which he has brought in, emptying the contents on the desk during the following)

Claude Patterson died at the hands of person or persons unknown. All I've got is the junk the old man was carrying in his pockets when they found the body. *(Handling the items)* Checks . . . Seventeen one-dollar bills . . . Ball-point pen . . . A snuff box . . . Wallet . . . Usual stuff. Driver's license . . . Photograph of a young girl, taken forty years ago, at least.

BARD

(Examining checks)

Checks made out to Claude Patterson, some to cash. Thirteen for three dollars, two for six bucks.

WINSTON

The guy made more'n I do.

CARSON

Some scraps of paper . . .
(BARD smoothes them out during the following.)

WINSTON

(To CARSON)

How long ago do they figure it happened?

CARSON

Before noon, coroner said. Old man must've run into the woods from the truck. A hunter came across the body just before dusk. City police found the truck parked alongside a service station other side of . . .

BARD

(Very, very quietly)
Hold it. *(Low whistle of amazement between teeth)* God.
Look't this . . . *(As others examine the scrap of paper)* State's
attorney's office examined this stuff?

CARSON

(As he looks at paper)
That was my impression. *(Then softly, too)* Good Lord!

WINSTON

(An excited whisper)
Patterson might've got just a quick glance. In a hurry,
y'know . . .

FREDERICKS

(Cynically)
He heard it on the radio . . . jotted it down just in case.

WINSTON

But if you change that 3 to a 8, you got it. Maybe his eyes
. . . a old man like that . . .

BARD

(Thoughtfully)
Or there was mud on the plate.

WINSTON

Jesse, if you change that 3 to a 8, you got it!

BARD

(With throb in voice)
Just for a while . . . just for a little while now . . . we're
going to change that 3 to an 8. We'll just kinda pretend Mr.
Patterson didn't *own* a radio. We're gonna pretend he saw

that license. Tom . . . these checks. Start working backwards! (*As* WINSTON *rises*) Names, addresses, telephone numbers, where they work. Everything!

FREDERICKS

Sure, let's go on a wild-goose chase . . . break the monotony.

BARD

Those were the last people saw him alive. These and whatever other customers live in that neighborhood. Let's find that neighborhood and let's scour it down with a wire brush.

WINSTON

Go ahead, Jess, say it.

BARD

I don't like to say it, Tom . . .

WINSTON

Say it, Jess. (*To* CARSON *as he exits*) He was right. . . . This is it!

BARD

God, it might be. Right here in town!

FREDERICKS

You want any more troopers on it, lemme know. My men got nothing else to do.
(*He exits.*)

BARD

(*Sitting at the desk*)
Any bets now, Carson? Any bets that beat-up gray car isn't in that neighborhood somewhere? Any bets, Harry?

113

CARSON

No bets, Jess.

BARD
(Flips intercom, speaks into it)
Dutch. Get me a city map in here. And a city directory!
(Flips off intercom. To CARSON*)* Now. If only we can get to
'em before some other innocent citizen stumbles across their
path . . .

(Blackout)

HILLIARD HOME

Evening. Living-room lights are on. Light in
RALPHIE'S *room is on. The door chimes sound.* ELEANOR
stands facing the door. GLENN *is moving from the win-*
dow to the stairs. HANK *is in door of den, automatic*
ready. Above, RALPHIE *sits on his bed with a small toy.*
The door chime is heard a second time.

GLENN

Okay, lady, answer it. But careful.
(He goes up the stairs until he is out of sight of the
front door. ELEANOR *looks at* HANK, *then goes to the*
front door and unlocks and opens it slightly. MISS
SWIFT *barges right in and* HANK *ducks into the den*
and closes the door, leaving it open enough to hear
and also cover the people in the room. GLENN *moves*
around the bend of the landing and stands near the
head of the stairs, listening. MISS SWIFT *is youngish,*
pert.)

MISS SWIFT

(As she pushes into the room)
Good evening, Mrs. Hilliard, I've come to see Ralph.

114

ELEANOR

(*Standing with the door open wide*)

Oh . . . yes. (*Glances nervously upstairs*) Yes . . . (*Speaks for* GLENN's *benefit*) Ralphie, it's your teacher. Miss Swift.

(ELEANOR *closes the door. Upstairs,* RALPHIE *opens the door of his room and starts down the hall; but, seeing* GLENN, *he returns to his room and stands listening at the door.*)

MISS SWIFT

(*As she moves down*)

You see, Ralph so rarely misses a day at school that I thought I'd drop by to . . . (*She stops, looking at the disordered room; her manner changes*) I . . . I daresay I should have telephoned first.

ELEANOR

(*Nervously*)

Oh, no, no, that's perfectly all . . . (*Abruptly*) Please sit down.

MISS SWIFT

(*Sits on sofa*)

I do hope that Ralph isn't seriously ill . . .

(*She realizes that she is sitting on an uncomfortable object, reaches back and brings out the empty whisky bottle, which she places on the coffee table.*)

ELEANOR

(*With a valiant effort at control*)

Only . . . just a cold. But we thought it best not to expose the other children.

(*Above,* RALPHIE *turns from the door of his room, picks up a composition book and a pencil from the bookshelves beside the bed. He sits in the chair writing in the composition book through the following.*)

MISS SWIFT

My dear Mrs. Hilliard, there is no such thing as a cold. Have you had a doctor's opinion?

ELEANOR

No. That is, we thought we could doctor it ourselves. . . .

MISS SWIFT

Mrs. Hilliard, how could you *possibly* doctor it yourself if you're convinced it's a *cold?* One member of a class stays home one day, and whoosh, it goes through the entire room. Not the germs, you understand, but the *idea* of the germs. (*She rises and moves quickly to stairs*) Perhaps I'd better have a look at him myself.

> (GLENN *quickly ducks out of sight and down the back stairs.* ELEANOR *moves fast and stops* MISS SWIFT *on the third step.*)

ELEANOR

No, you can't!

RALPHIE

(*Calling from his room*)
I'll be down in a minute, Miss Swift!

MISS SWIFT

Well, of course, if I've come . . .

RALPHIE

I'm just finishing my composition!

MISS SWIFT

(*Smiling*)
Your son, Mrs. Hilliard, is going to be a brilliant author some day. . . . (CINDY *enters through front door, followed by* DAN *and* ROBISH) You mark my . . . (*She breaks off as she sees* DAN) Mr. Hilliard?

(CINDY *stops.* ROBISH, *after one glance at* MISS SWIFT, *closes the door and stands against the frame with his back to her.*)

ELEANOR

Dan, you . . . uh . . . remember Miss Swift. Ralphie's *teacher!* (DAN *glances from den to rear hall, immediately alert*) Ralphie, are you *coming?*

DAN

Sure I remember. How're you, Miss Swift?

ELEANOR

Miss Swift . . . dropped in to see how Ralphie was feeling. (*As* MISS SWIFT *stares at* DAN, *he makes his decision. He is drunk! He immediately goes into a muted drunk act, turns to* ROBISH.)

DAN

She did, did she? What do you think of that . . . Johnny? That's what I call a nice little old PTA practice. (*Ushering* ROBISH *toward the dining room*) You know where I keep it, Johnny. Help yourself. (MISS SWIFT *stares at* ROBISH *as he, keeping his face turned away from her, moves into the dining room. He turns, when out of her line of vision, and draws the .38 from his pocket as the dining-room door closes.* DAN *grabs* MISS SWIFT *by the arm, turning her away from* ROBISH) Miss Swift! Met old pal Johnny at a . . . (*Turns to* CINDY) Cindy, say hello to Miss Swift. (CINDY *and* MISS SWIFT *exchange nods.* DAN *sits on sofa*) Whew, has Cindy been laying it to me! Leave it to Cindy to know where to find her old man.

(ROBISH *appears in pantry, speaks to* GLENN, *who is listening. Above,* RALPHIE *starts down the stairs.*)

ROBISH

She seen me!

GLENN

Clam up!

DAN

(*Picks up whisky bottle from coffee table and upends it into coffee cup*)
Where does the stuff go in this house?
(*He lays the bottle flat on the coffee table.*)

RALPHIE

(*On stair, one step above* MISS SWIFT)
I . . . I finished my composition for this week, Miss Swift.

MISS SWIFT

(*Nonplused, takes composition book*)
I'll . . . I'll see that you get full credit, Ralph.
(*She turns and steps down one step, but* DAN *stops her.*)

DAN

(*In a commanding tone*)
Miss Swift! (*He rises and goes to foot of stairs*) I'll take that, please. (*He takes the composition book from her hands rudely, opens it and reads, then looks up at* RALPHIE, *who turns and runs up the stairs and into his own room, where he stands listening at the partly closed door*) So . . . so this is what they call a composition nowadays. You . . . you encourage such drivel, Miss Swift?

MISS SWIFT

Mr. Hilliard . . . in all fairness . . . I don't think you're in any condition to discuss *anything* tonight.

DAN

In that case, I'll read it in the morning.
(MISS SWIFT *glances upstairs, then comes down and crosses to* ELEANOR, *places a hand on her arm.*)

118

MISS SWIFT

Mrs. Hilliard, let me assure you that what I've seen here tonight will in no way affect my belief in Ralph.

(*After a glance back at* DAN, *she goes quickly to the front door, opens it, and marches out, closing the door. Immediately,* HANK *rushes in from the den and up to the front door and locks it, then moves to the window and stands looking out.* ELEANOR *crosses toward* DAN, *who sinks into the chair.* ROBISH *enters from the dining room, followed by* GLENN.)

ELEANOR

Oh, Dan . . . Dan, how did you ever? . . .

ROBISH

Griffin, we gotta stop that dame!

HANK

Sure, Robish . . . shoot up the whole town!

ROBISH

She seen *me!*

DAN

She wasn't looking at you!

GLENN

Old guy's right, Robish. Hilliard took her mind offa you. Stand up, Pop! (DAN *rises and* GLENN *frisks him*) Gotta hand it to you, Hilliard. You had that dame in a real stew. You'd of made a great con man. (*To* ELEANOR) Get up there with that smart brat.

(ELEANOR *turns and goes up the stairs.*)

HANK

Glenn . . . this is goin' on too long.

GLENN

(*Ignoring* HANK)

Robish, did you get that piece of paper outta the old guy's pocket?

ROBISH

Couldn't. He jumped outta the truck.

GLENN

You dumb goddam . . .

ROBISH

(*Displaying the pistol*)

He didn't get far.

GLENN

(*Reaching for it*)

I'll take the .38 now, Robish.

ROBISH

(*Holds it away*)

I kinda like th' feel of it.

(*Pause . . . a silent duel.*)

GLENN

(*An effort to hold his command*)

Get on the back door.

ROBISH

Get on the back door yourself, Griffin. Stuff it!

(ROBISH *laughs defiantly, pockets the gun and sits.*)

DAN

Griffin . . . the money didn't come to the office today.

GLENN
(*His mind on* ROBISH *and the gun*)
Dope it yourself, Pop, you're so smart.

DAN
You didn't really expect it.

GLENN
Mail takes time. You should-a thought of that. It wasn't mailed till early this mornin. (*Grinning, turns to* DAN) Ought to get here some time tomorrow.
(*Pause. General shock.*)

HANK
(*Bleakly*)
Tomorrow?

DAN
(*To* GLENN—*angrily*)
Why, you young . . .

GLENN
Take it easy, Pop . . . 'n stay healthy. (*To* HANK) Yeah . . . tomorrow. What's one more night?

HANK
(*Low*)
Christ!

DAN
Griffin, I've played your filthy game up to now . . . but by bringing that ape back here after he killed a man . . .

ROBISH
(*Threatening, under his breath*)
Who you callin' a ape?

DAN

. . . we're accessories now.

GLENN

That's right, Hilliard. You're on our side now. (*To* HANK) I'll take the automatic, kid.

HANK

(*Takes a backward step away from* GLENN)
I'm hanging onto it.
(HANK *turns and exits through the dining-room door and goes into the pantry, where he stands looking out the window of the side door.* GLENN *steps to the dining-room door, stops, and turns back to* DAN.)

GLENN

How you like that, Pop? They both got the guns. (*Raises his voice so* HANK *can hear in the pantry*) Only they ain't got half a brain between 'em. Without me, they're cooked . . . an' they know it. (GLENN *turns on* CINDY, *moving toward her*) You didn't feel like blabberin' to the boy friend, did you, sweetie?

CINDY

(*Holding her ground*)
I felt like it. But I didn't. I'll explain it the night you take your walk to the electric chair.
(GLENN's *tension has been growing. He explodes.* HANK *turns from the pantry window and rushes into the living room.*)

GLENN

(*Threateningly, to* CINDY, *who backs away*)
There're ways of shuttin' that pretty face of yours, redhead!

HANK

(*As he enters the living room*)

What's the boy friend doin' drivin' past the house out there . . . slow?

GLENN

(*Pushing her shoulder, forces her against window*)

If you pulled a fast one, spitfire . . .

HANK

(*In panic*)

Glenn, listen!

GLENN

(*Turning back into room*)

Lemme think, willya?

HANK

Glenn! They're not gonna stop comin' to the door!

GLENN

(*Crossing to him*)

Yellow, Hank?

HANK

Yeah . . . okay . . . yellow! *They're not gonna stop coming to the door!*

(*Blackout*)

SHERIFF'S OFFICE

Clock: 8:25. There is a map of Indianapolis on the wall and an area has been marked off with heavy crayon. FREDERICKS *is studying the map.* BARD *is speaking over the radio.*

123

BARD

I'm looking at a map of the neighborhood, Tom. Where are you?

WINSTON'S VOICE

Parked behind a service station. Corner of Kessler Boulevard and Keystone. (*As* BARD *marks an X on the map location*) The main roads are covered. The other cars're just where you put 'em. It's a high-toned sort of neighborhood, Jess.

BARD

Okay. Now. Let's start knocking on a few high-toned doors!

FREDERICKS

Bard . . . there're over two hundred houses in that area. It'll take all night and part of tomorrow. . . .

BARD
(*Ignoring* FREDERICKS)
Every one of the trashman's customers. Begin with those. And Tom . . . especially the garages, you got me?
(CARSON *enters.*)

WINSTON'S VOICE

We're on it, Jess. . . .
(BARD *switches off the radio.*)

CARSON
(*Holding out letter*)
This, my friend, was brought into the city police station during the noon hour.

BARD
(*Taking the letter*)
Noon!

124

CARSON

A bellhop's given six different descriptions of the man who tipped him five bucks to deliver it. All we know for sure is the man had two arms, two legs and presumably one head.

BARD

(Takes letter out of envelope, glances at it)
It's not signed.

CARSON

Go ahead, read it . . . you'll understand why.

BARD

(Begins to read briskly . . . and tone changes to a hushed whisper)
"To the Police . . . innocent people will be in the house or automobile with the three fugitives you want. If you shoot, you will be responsible for taking the lives of people who have done no harm. Any attempt to trace this letter will only endanger my family. . . ." *(Pause. BARD holds letter up to light)* Handwriting disguised . . . no watermarks.

FREDERICKS

It's a blind.

BARD

(Whisper . . . touched)
The idiot.

CARSON

That letter's no blind.

BARD

But he ought to *know!* God, doesn't he know? Carson, isn't there some way to get word to this guy, whoever he is, that you can't play ball with savages like that?

125

CARSON

How? Without tipping them he wrote that?

BARD

You take a shot in the dark, Federal man! They'll tear that poor guy to ribbons, inside and out, before they're done. You can't co-operate with scum like that!

CARSON

No? . . . What would *you* do, Jesse? I'd say he was smart to write that. Might keep some itchy-fingered officer from shooting his wife or child.

BARD

Itchy-fingered like me, Carson?

CARSON

You got more sense. That's what's eating you, friend. You know what a spot the man's on. What *would* you do, Jesse . . . under the circumstances?

BARD

(*After a moment*)
I'd play ball. (BARD *flips on intercom and speaks into it*) Dutch, get me car nine . . . Deputy Winston. (*Flips off the intercom. Quietly*) Yeah, I reckon I'd do just that. An' maybe pray a little.
(BARD *switches on radio circuit light.*)

WINSTON'S VOICE

Car nine . . .

BARD

Tom . . . stop 'em up there.

126

WINSTON'S VOICE
(*Incredulously*)

Stop 'em . . . ?

BARD

You heard me. I'm countermanding the orders. Bury those prowl cars, *bury* 'em.

FREDERICKS

You can't put off a showdown, lad.

BARD

Nobody wants a showdown any more'n I do . . . but not if it means getting some poor slob's family massacred! (*Into mike*) You hear me, Tom? Keep those patrols off the streets! Stash 'em!

WINSTON'S VOICE

You're callin' it, Jess. . . . Listen—that sporty little foreign car I reported a while ago . . . he just went by the corner again.

BARD

(*Considers a moment*)
Okay. Bring him in, Tom. Who knows? But quiet up there! No sirens, no red lights.

WINSTON'S VOICE

It'll be a pleasure to arrest *any*body!
(BARD *switches off the radio.*)

FREDERICKS

You call that police work?

BARD

What do you propose . . . alert 'em, force their hand?

FREDERICKS

That letter pretty well establishes they're in that neighborhood. I'll tell you what I propose—tear gas.

BARD

Anybody wonder why this guy didn't sign his name? Why he doesn't trust the police to help him?

FREDERICKS

Tear gas and riot guns. I'll have some moved up there . . . just in case you begin to see the light!
(FREDERICKS *exits. Pause.*)

CARSON
(Quietly)
Changing your tune, Jess? . . .
(BARD *moves to the desk, puzzled at himself and his feelings, ignores* CARSON. *He rereads the letter in silence.*)

BARD

Those guys wouldn't try to use a sports car for a getaway. Probably some fresh kid out trying to pick up a girl. . . .

(Blackout)

HILLIARD HOME

The living-room lights are on, the rest of the house dim. ELEANOR *is with* RALPHIE *in his room.* DAN *is seated in the living room.* ROBISH *is at door of den.* CINDY *is on the second step of the stairs.* HANK *is at the window.* GLENN *is at the front door, which is very slightly ajar so that he can look out through the crack.*

HANK

He knows somethin's up. . . .

CINDY

Chuck knows nothing. Naturally, he's puzzled . . . he . . .

GLENN

(*Closes and locks the door*)
Knock off, I'm thinkin'.

HANK

Glenn . . .

GLENN

(*Abstracted*)
Don't let it get you, kid.

HANK

Glenn . . . I've had it.

GLENN

What're you talkin' about?

HANK

The old man with the trash . . . the teacher . . . now
this guy goin' by out there . . . over'n over. I've had it.
(*He goes into the dining room and to the pantry,
where he stands looking out the window of the side
door.*)

GLENN

(*Moving fast to the dining room*)
Robish, cover 'em!
(ROBISH *rises and glances out window.*)

GLENN

(*Enters the pantry, grabs* HANK's *arm*)
What the hell does that mean? "I've had it"?

HANK

What're we waitin' for, Glenn?

129

GLENN

Don't start that again! I gotta dope this . . .

HANK

We're accessories now.
(DAN *rises and leaves the living-room by the dining-room door.* CINDY *moves to the dining-room door, listening.*)

GLENN

You're learnin' big words aroun' this house, ain't you?

HANK

Glenn . . . I ain't going to the chair 'cause that ape in there got trigger happy.

GLENN

We're pullin' stakes tomorrow . . . *after* we get the dough.
(DAN *appears in the pantry.*)

HANK
(*Shouting*)
What good's the dough gonna do you in the death house?

GLENN
(*Intensely*)
I gotta pay Flick to take care of Bard, don't I? (*Turns, following* HANK's *gaze, sees* DAN) What're you gapin' at?

HANK

I'm goin', Glenn. By myself.

GLENN
(*Whirling on him*)
You leave here without me, they'll have you back'n stir'n less'n a hour.

HANK

I can take care of myself.

GLENN

Since when?

HANK

(*Firmly*)

Since right now!
        (GLENN *is baffled, angry, frightened, unable to cope.*)

GLENN

Listen, you yellow little punk . . . you're gonna do what
I tell you!

HANK

Not any more, Glenn.

DAN

Hank, I don't advise your leaving here alone. . . .

HANK

They won't catch me, Mr. Hilliard. Don't worry about that.

GLENN

(*Between them*)

Look who's tellin' who not to worry! You're talkin' like
Hilliard was our old man. (*Faces* DAN) If Hilliard was our old
man, he'd have something coming to him from way back!
(HANK *unlocks the door and* GLENN *whips about . . . changing: pleading now, helpless, slightly pathetic*) Listen, Hank
. . . you can't duck out on me. Christ, kid . . . it's always
been *us.* You'n me. Listen . . . without you . . . without
you . . .

HANK

Come along, Glenn?

131

GLENN

(*Wildly*)

Goddammit, I'm callin' the tune! You're gonna listen to me, I took care of you, I . . .

(GLENN *breaks off because* HANK *has taken the automatic from his pocket.* GLENN *stares.*)

HANK

You ain't stoppin' me . . . either one of you. (*Pause*) I'll take the girl's coop.

(CINDY, *who has been standing at the dining-room door, now slips out, heading for the pantry.*)

DAN

(*Quickly*)

They could trace that license in ten minutes.

HANK

Okay, Mr. Hilliard . . . I can pick up a car anywhere.

ROBISH

(*Calls to* GLENN)

Griffin . . . redhead's gettin' nosy!

(CINDY *appears in the pantry.* HANK *sees her, and on his face is the naked longing.* GLENN *turns, frowning . . . he sees* CINDY. *He taps his forehead with the heel of his hand, smiling.*)

GLENN

I get it. Christ, kid, I get it now! (*He grabs* CINDY *and pulls her toward* HANK. DAN *puts his arm around her, holding* GLENN *off*) Ain't I always learned you? You want something, take it!

DAN

Your brother knows it's not that simple, Griffin!

GLENN

(*Fiercely*)

I'll *make* it that simple! *Hank gets what he wants!*
(*Pause . . . while* HANK *looks at* CINDY.)

HANK

(*In choked tones*)

I doubt it, Glenn. I doubt if I ever will.
(HANK *suddenly opens the door, turns and goes out, slamming the door behind him. He quickly disappears.* GLENN *springs to the door and looks out the window. Stunned, muttering almost to himself, he sags in door.*)

GLENN

You be careful, kid. . . . Take care of yourself, see . . . You . . . (*He turns and sees* CINDY *in* DAN's *arms, pulls up the swagger*) Good riddance. He was beginnin' to get on my nerves. (*Then, abruptly*) You satisfied, redhead?

DAN

Cindy had nothing to do with . . .

GLENN

Satisfied?

DAN

Go to your room, Cindy. (CINDY *slips up the back stairs.* DAN *turns to* GLENN, *who goes toward the living room, seething, growing more and more violent.* DAN *follows* GLENN) Griffin, you'd better get hold of yourself.
(*Above,* ELEANOR *has left* RALPHIE *and is now at the head of the stairs.*)

ELEANOR

Dan, what is it? What . . .

133

GLENN

(*As he enters the living room*)

All of you. All of you! (*Turns on* DAN) You satisfied now, you smart-eyed bastard? Clickety-click, you got at him, didn't you?

(*Above,* RALPHIE *joins* ELEANOR *at head of stairs.*)

DAN

God, boy, you'd better . . .

GLENN

Shut up, Pop! . . . Pop! If you was our pop . . .

DAN

Griffin, I don't know how much reason you've got left in that head of yours, but you can't turn this on . . .

GLENN

(*Pacing like a maddened caged animal*)

I can do anything I want! You and your goddam house!

ROBISH

(*At window*)

Stir-crazy!

GLENN

That goddam spitfire'n her fancy skirts swishin'!

DAN

I'd advise you to let loose of that idea!

GLENN

(*Grabs composition book from table and sweeps ash tray to the floor*)

That brat an' his "composition"!

DAN

(*Still at foot of stairs*)
If you don't get hold . . .
(ELEANOR *comes down the stairs a few steps.*)

GLENN

I got hold! I got hold good! (*Twisting the composition book in his hands*) Now I'm gonna "advise" you, Pop. You're gonna go up there now an' you're gonna learn that kid we ain't playin' cowboys-an'-Indians aroun' here. (*Taking pleasure in it*) You're gonna give that brat a real old-fashioned lacin'.

DAN

We don't do things that way in this house!

GLENN

This house, this house! I got my gut-full-a this house! (*Eyes on* DAN) Robish! How'd *you* like to show Hilliard how it's done?

ROBISH

Yeah . . . I ain't got nothin' else to do.
(*Above,* RALPHIE *returns to his own room, stands by bed.*)

GLENN

(*Sadistically*)
Okay, Robish . . . whale the tar outta that brat!
(ROBISH *starts to the stairs.* DAN *moves up the stairs slowly.* ROBISH *stops at foot of stairs.*)

ELEANOR

(*Leaning on stair rail. To* GLENN)
I hope they get your brother! I hope they kill him!

GLENN

(*Calls up to* DAN)

Let's hear him bawlin', Pop! *Loud.* My old man used a belt!
(DAN *enters* RALPHIE's *room, closes the door and turns on the light.* ELEANOR *mounts the stairs and goes into the master bedroom, where she stands listening behind the closed door.* DAN *faces* RALPHIE.)

DAN

(*Breathlessly*)

Ralphie . . .

RALPHIE

Did Hank take your gun? Then there's only one gun now. . . .

DAN

(*Gently, but urgently*)

Son . . . you've got to help. . . .

ROBISH

(*Starts up the stairs*)

We don't hear nothin', Hilliard!

DAN

(*Swiftly, softly, suffering*)

Ralphie . . . listen to me. No matter what you think now . . . no matter what you think of me . . . what names you give it . . . you've got to do what I tell you.

ROBISH

(*Rounding the landing*)

What's goin' on in there?

DAN

Ralphie, listen! I want you to cry.

136

ROBISH

(Coming down the hall)

What's the stall?

DAN

(Almost a whisper)

Do you hear me? Ralphie . . . son . . . please . . . for God's sake do what I say now.

RALPHIE

I . . . I can't.

ROBISH

(Outside the door)

You want some help, Hilliard?

(Trapped, DAN lifts his hand and brings it down, in desperation, open-palmed: a stinging blow across the boy's face. RALPHIE, stunned, stands staring at his father. DAN goes sick and empty clear through. Then DAN sinks to bed, gathers RALPHIE in his arms, and RALPHIE begins to cry. He cries softly at first, then louder and louder. Below, GLENN hears the sounds and drops the composition book to the floor, as though he has found some small release inside.)

(Dimout)

SHERIFF'S OFFICE

Clock reads 8:59. WINSTON stands to one side of CHUCK, who, bewildered, faces BARD across the desk. BARD is examining CHUCK's driver's license.

BARD

What's your business, Mr. . . . (Glances at license) Wright?

CHUCK

Attorney, Swisshelm and Edwards. Circle Tower Building.
... What's this all about?

BARD

Your firm handle criminal cases?

CHUCK

We're strictly corporation law. You haven't answered my
question, Deputy.

WINSTON

Don't get fresh.

BARD

Empty out your pockets, Wright.

CHUCK

You've no right to ...

BARD

Look, Wright . . . you're not in court! Empty out your
pockets! (*As* CHUCK *complies*) What you been up to, last hour
or so . . . in that . . . (*Consults* CHUCK's *registration*) Jaguar of
yours? Cruising round in circles?

WINSTON

You scoutin' for those rats, Wright?

CHUCK

What rats?

BARD

Let's not be cagey, kid . . . it makes me suspicious. (*Picks
up newspaper from top of radio and hands it to* CHUCK, *who
reads the headlines and begins to realize* . . .) We know
they're up there somewhere . . . holed up in one of those nice
houses . . . so . . . (*Stops, frowning . . . studying expression on*
CHUCK's *face*) What's up, boy?

CHUCK

Nothing . . .

BARD

You know something? (*When* CHUCK *shakes his head*) Suspect something?

CHUCK

No . . .

BARD

(*Rising*)

Dammit, don't lie to me! Your face looks like I just kicked you.

CHUCK

Well . . . it's just that . . . my girl lives . . . there.

BARD

Name?

CHUCK

Her name's . . . Allen (*Firmly*) Constance Allen.

WINSTON

(*Consulting the list*)

No Allens on the list, Jess.

BARD

(*Picks up* DAN's *letter, hands it to* CHUCK)

Here . . . read this. (BARD SITS *as* CHUCK *reads*) Now. Let's have it, kid. What's the girl's name?

CHUCK

I . . . don't know.

BARD

(*Gently probing now*)

She's in there . . . with those three. What's the address?

CHUCK

If . . . if he'd wanted you to know . . . (*Tosses letter to the desk*) he'd have signed his name.

BARD

(*Changing*)

Wright, that guy ought to know he can't cribbage aroun' with the police like this. If he doesn't, you should!

CHUCK

What do you expect him to do? He's doing all he can! He's quite a guy!

BARD

(*Rising*)

Kid . . . I honestly don't know what I'd do if I was in your shoes . . . but I'm in mine . . . and I want that name. Now spit it out or I'll slap you in the pokey so fast . . .

CHUCK

You've got no charges!

BARD

I've got sixty of 'em. Aidin' and abettin' . . . withholding evidence . . . accessory to murder! Or didn't you know they murdered a man this afternoon? Yeah, that's the kind of scum you're lettin' your girl spend the evening with.
(*Pause.* CHUCK *sinks into chair.* BARD *sits on edge of desk.* CHUCK *swallows.*)

CHUCK

I . . . I can't make that decision. For them. You'd better slap on one of those charges, Deputy. Because I don't know the name. I never said I did.

BARD
(Rising)
Why, you young . . .
    (He is interrupted by the intercom.)

DUTCH'S VOICE
Special Agent Carson, Jesse.

BARD
(Switches on radio)
Yes, Carson?

CARSON'S VOICE
Deputy . . . it just blew wide open!

BARD
What? . . . What've you got?

CARSON'S VOICE
City policemen just caught Hank Griffin trying to steal a car. He decided to shoot it out. . . .

BARD
Killed?

CARSON'S VOICE
Killed.

BARD
(In a different tone . . . very quietly)
Anything else?

CARSON'S VOICE
Plenty . . . The gun the boy was carrying—it was registered. *(As* BARD's *eyes meet* CHUCK's) In the name of Hilliard . . . Daniel C. Hilliard.
    *(*BARD *glances at* WINSTON, *who glances at list, looks up, nods.)*

BARD

Just like that. Eleanor Hilliard wrote a check to Claude Patterson this morning.

WINSTON

(Reading from list)

Hilliard, Daniel C. Wife, Eleanor. One son age ten, Ralph. One daughter age twenty, Cynthia . . . called Cindy.

(CHUCK *has turned in the chair, watching* WINSTON. *Their eyes now meet.*)

BARD

(After a slight pause)

Okay. Carson . . . throw a cordon around the Hilliard house. Let no one in or out of that block. Only keep everything out of sight of the windows. I'll be up there in ten minutes. And Carson . . . have the newsboys got this?

CARSON'S VOICE

Not yet. Not even the death.

BARD

Well, for god's sake, keep 'em off it!

CARSON'S VOICE

We'll try, Jess.

(BARD *flips off the radio circuit light.*)

WINSTON

(Gets coat)

You call it, Jess.

CHUCK

(Rising)

You can't move in! You read Mr. Hilliard's letter.

BARD

(*Taking his revolver out of desk drawer, checks it. Abstracted*)
Get out of here now, kid.

CHUCK

(*Demanding*)
What're you going to do?

BARD

What the sweet hell do you think I'm going to do ... blow
up the house?
    (BARD *takes his jacket from back of chair and starts
    putting it on.*)

CHUCK

(*Earnestly*)
Deputy ... what if you could sneak someone inside? With
a gun. There are only two of them in there now.

WINSTON

(*Putting on coat*)
This is police work, son. Stay out of it.

CHUCK

If somebody was in there ... between them and the family
... and if he could get 'em both at one crack ...

BARD

(*Ignoring* CHUCK, *flips on intercom*)
Dutch ... get an ambulance up to Kessler and Keystone.
Keep it out of sight. (*Flips off intercom. Turns to* CHUCK)
You're out of it, Wright. Stay out!

CHUCK

I'm not out of it! Those're my people in there! (*To* BARD,
urgently) You read the letter. There can't be any shooting
when they come out, either. .... *What are you going to do?*

BARD

(*Annoyed at the question*)
Look! Will you get out of here!

CHUCK

May I have my things?

BARD

(*Shoving items across the desk*)
Take 'em.

CHUCK

(*Picking up his things, putting them in pockets*)
May I have those keys, Deputy?

BARD

(*Looks at keys, which he has unconsciously been holding in his hand since he went through* CHUCK's *belongings*)
Here.
(*He hands the keys to* CHUCK.)

CHUCK

Thanks.
(CHUCK *goes out, as* WINSTON *returns with rifle.*)

WINSTON

The boy's got a good question, Jess.

BARD

(*Thoughtfully; quietly*)
A damn good question . . . I wish I had the answer. (*As they start out*) Well, let's get on it now. Let's get up there!

(*Dimout*)

Curtain

ACT THREE

ACT THREE

DAN *is at the window of the master bedroom.* ELEA-
NOR *is sitting on the bed. Across the hall,* RALPHIE *is
asleep on his bed.* CINDY *is out of sight in her room.*
ROBISH *is at the window in the living room.* GLENN *is
in the pantry. As the lights dim up he is leaving the
pantry and appears in the living room. Living-room
lights are on; the rest of the house is dim.*

ROBISH
(Turning from the window as GLENN *enters)*
Griffin . . . somethin' funny goin' on. There ain't been no
cars goin' by out there for a long time. *(Steps toward* GLENN*)*
Griffin, you deef?

GLENN
(Who has been pacing, stops)
Robish . . . let's grab the two women'n blow.

ROBISH

With no dough?

GLENN
(Vacantly)
With no dough.

ROBISH

Okay. Ya wanna go . . . go. Wind up like the kid brother.
In the morgue.

GLENN

Lay off, Robish.

147

ROBISH

On a slab. By this time they got 'im or shot 'im.
(*Above,* DAN *goes to other window in the bedroom.*)

GLENN
(*Wildly*)
Nothin' happens to Hank!

ROBISH
(*Chuckles heavily*)
That's po'try, Griffin. Got 'im or shot 'im.

GLENN
(*Starting toward* ROBISH)
You don't know nothin'! Goddam you, Robish . . .
(ROBISH *lifts the gun, almost casually. In this moment,
the telephone shrills.* GLENN *stops.*)

ROBISH
(*Shouting*)
Hilliard! Answer that!
(DAN *turns on the bedroom lights, opens the door, and
picks up the phone in the upstairs hall at the time that*
GLENN, *below, is already answering it.* CINDY *has come
out of her room and stands near the door to* RALPHIE'S
room, DAN, *undecided as to what to do with the phone,
looks at* CINDY.)

GLENN
(*Leaping to the phone almost before the first ring is over*)
Hank! (*Into instrument*) Hello! (*Then, sagging in disap-
pointment, snarls*) Who? . . .
(*He replaces the phone angrily.*)

ROBISH
(*Approaching* GLENN)
Christ, *who is it?*

GLENN

(Vacantly, going through dining-room door)
Something about . . . a night watchman . . .

ROBISH

(Calling)

Hilliard!

DAN

(Speaks into the extension)
Hello . . . this is Mr. Hilliard speaking. *(Suddenly alert)*
Yes, Carl? . . . I'll be right down.
(DAN replaces the phone and turns to the stairs.)

ROBISH

(At foot of stairs)
Who was that? What's going on?

DAN

(On stairs, calls down)
The money's here. It arrived special delivery at the store.
I'll go get it.
*(DAN turns back up the stairs and enters the bedroom,
where he faces ELEANOR, who is sitting on the bed.
CINDY returns to her own room. GLENN has returned
from the dining room during DAN's last speech. ROBISH
turns to him.)*

ROBISH

(Trying to penetrate GLENN's preoccupation)
Griffin . . . the dough's here.

GLENN

(Stands for a moment at foot of stairs)
How come that wasn't Hank on the phone?

149

ROBISH

You better snap out of it. (*As* GLENN *goes into the den*) Jeez, you're givin' me the willies. . . .

(*He stands looking after* GLENN. *In the bedroom above,* DAN *picks up his coat from over the back of the chair and paces with the coat in his hands.* ELEANOR *follows him with her eyes as she speaks.*)

ELEANOR

I can't believe it. Now. Tonight! No more waiting. In an hour now .. . *Less* than an hour! (*Slight pause.* DAN *puts on his coat*) Dan . . . look at me. . . . (*Rises, fighting alarm*) Dan!

ROBISH
(*Shouting up the stairs*)
Hilliard! That dough's waiting!

ELEANOR

Tell me. What are you planning, Dan?
(*Pause.* DAN *turns to face her.*)

DAN

I can't wait any longer for the opportune moment, that's all.

ELEANOR

What do you mean?

DAN

I've got to . . . make the moment . . . for myself.

ELEANOR
(*Sinks down at foot of bed*)
Dan, tell me. My blood's stopped. Dan . . .

DAN

There are only three bullets left in that gun down there.

ELEANOR

I'm going to scream!

DAN

No you're not, you're going to listen.

ELEANOR

My heart's pushing up out of . . . Dan, *what do you mean?*

DAN

I'm going to force Robish to use those bullets.

ELEANOR
(*Whispers*)

Use them . . . How?

DAN
(*Quietly*)

On me.

ROBISH

Hilliard, what's the stall?

ELEANOR
(*Rising, to him*)

Dan, this isn't you. They've driven you . . . Oh, God, *Dan!*

DAN

I've tried every other way, haven't I? *Haven't* I?

ELEANOR
(*Swiftly . . . in a whisper*)

We know, we're not asking for more, we know what you've done. Even Ralphie . . .

DAN

If I can get Griffin out of the way before Robish even knows what's happening . . . (*Grimly; murderously*) And I *can.*

ELEANOR

Dan, no matter how much you want to kill Griffin . . .

DAN

There's no other way!

ELEANOR

There is. There has to be!

DAN

(*Gently, urgently*)

Darling, you've got to face this with me. Griffin hates me. He hated me before he even saw me. I can't explain it. Every hour some new black hole appears in him. He's cracking up, Ellie. God knows what a mind like that will turn to . . . which one of us . . . Now. Do you see? We're no better off when I get the money. Do you see?

ELEANOR

All I see is one thing. One thing . . . *We're* not saved if *you* die.

DAN

Please, Ellie, don't make it so . . .

ELEANOR

All right . . . go down there. Kill Griffin. Make Robish shoot you. Do you imagine a man like that has to have *bullets* to . . . (DAN *turns to her*) against Ralphie? . . . or Cindy? . . . or me? *Do* you?

152

DAN

> *(Realizing that it was only panic, softly)*

All right, Ellie.

ELEANOR

We're not saved if you die.

DAN

All *right,* Ellie!

ELEANOR

> *(Sits on bed)*

Oh, God, darling. (DAN *sinks into chair*) Dan . . . you're the hub . . . it all revolves around you. If anything . . .

DAN

Everything's blurred again. One minute it all looks sharp . . . clear . . .

ELEANOR

> *(Places her hand on DAN's)*

Dan. (*He looks at her*) We can't let them panic us now.
> *(There is a moment of understanding between them.)*

ROBISH

Hilliard! Get th' lead out!
> (DAN *and* ELEANOR *break. He rises and opens the door, starting downstairs.* ELEANOR *rises and stands at the door.*)

GLENN

> *(Entering from den)*

Ask 'em where they get the news on that damn thing.
> (DAN *is coming down the stairs.* CINDY *comes out of her room and follows.* GLENN *sinks to chair.*)

153

ROBISH

Goddam you, Hilliard, you don't get down here, I'm gonna . . . (*He sees* DAN *on the stairs*) We ain't gonna blow till we get that dough, Hilliard.

GLENN

Where's the redhead?
(DAN, *moving to the closet, turns to* CINDY *on stairs.*)

DAN

Cindy, go to your room. Lock the door.

GLENN

Redhead goes along!
(CINDY *remains on the stairs.*)

ROBISH

(*Turning to* GLENN)
The gal stays right here.

GLENN

(*Ignoring* ROBISH—*a grotesque caricature of his old self*)
Open the letter . . . take out two thousand dollars . . .

ROBISH

To hell with that!

GLENN

Redhead takes it to Lombardi's Grille . . .

DAN

(*Putting on coat*)
Cindy is not going to deliver any . . .

GLENN

(*Turns in chair to face* DAN)
Lombardi Grille. South Illinois Street.

ROBISH

To hell with that. Ain't got time now!

GLENN

She sits'n has a drink. A man sits down with her. Then . . .

ROBISH

Then nothin'! Yuh lissen to me. . . .

GLENN

(*Vaguely*)

Then . . .

DAN

What then, Griffin?

GLENN

She gives him the dough. Two G's.

ROBISH

Yuh bring all that dough here, Hilliard . . . soon's yuh lay
your mitts on it.

(DAN *goes to open the door.*)

GLENN

We don't get outta here till I hear from Flick he's got his
money.

(DAN, *with door open, now nods to* CINDY, *who comes
down the stairs and goes out.* DAN *follows and closes
the door.*)

155

ROBISH

Wastin' time, wastin' time. I tell yuh the redhead stays. We gotta have ... (*He hears the door close. Turns*) Now, how we gonna take two dames in the car? (*He locks the door as* GLENN *goes to the phone, dials*) Loco. Christ! Loco.

(ROBISH *goes into pantry, locks the back door.*)

GLENN
(*On phone*)
What? ... Oh ... Mr. Flick. Room ... uh ... 202.

(ROBISH *returns to the living room.*)

ROBISH
(*In dining-room door*)
I lay my hands'n that dough, yuh can rot'n here, Griffin. . . .

(*Blackout*)

THE WALLINGS' ATTIC

The corner of an attic room that seems to be suspended in darkness. The room has a cluttered look: discarded furniture, an old iron bed-frame leaning against the wall. A single small window overlooks the Hilliard house in the distance. CARSON *is looking out the window through binoculars.* BARD *behind him, wearing hat.* FREDERICKS *is seated on an old trunk. On an old box is radio apparatus. A rifle with a telescopic sight leans against the wall near the window.*

CARSON
(*Reporting, without lowering binoculars*)
Jesse ... a man and a girl just came out the front door of the Hilliard house.

BARD
That'll be Hilliard and his daughter.

CARSON

They're getting into the black coupé in the driveway. (*He hands the glasses to* BARD, *who looks through the window*) Cocky, aren't they? Letting them both out of there even now.

BARD

Yeah . . . gettin' real cocksure.

FREDERICKS
(*Crisply*)

Why not? They know they got us hog-tied . . . 's long as we sit up here in the attic of the house next door.

BARD

(*Hands glasses back to* CARSON *and turns to* FREDERICKS)
Don't start riding me again, Fredericks.
> (*There is a buzz from the radio apparatus.* BARD *flips a switch and picks up the microphone.*)

WINSTON'S VOICE
(*On radio*)

Car nine—Winston.

BARD
(*Into mike*)

Yeah, Tom?

WINSTON'S VOICE

Jesse . . . Hilliard and his daughter just turned south on Keystone. You want me to pick 'em up?

BARD

No.

FREDERICKS

What the hell're we waitin' for? We got the phone tap. We know where he's going.

BARD

(Annoyed—into mike)

Tom . . . let them get downtown to that store. Then . . . when he's got his mail, whatever it is . . . pick him up and bring him here to the Wallings' house. Come in here from the north, though . . . and careful nobody in the Hilliard windows can see you.

WINSTON'S VOICE

What'll I tell the guy?

BARD

Nothing.
(Flips off radio, puts down mike.)

FREDERICKS

Bard, this is stupid as hell! I tell you, we got no choice now. Move in.

BARD

And I tell you I've got an animal gnawing away inside me tonight, Fredericks, and I don't need this crap from you! I'm aware of the alternatives. We could bust in there now . . . or try to bluff 'em out . . . or try to sneak in and flush 'em . . . but . . .

FREDERICKS

(Rising)

Let's get one thing straight. There's going to be blood. There're only two people in that house now.

BARD

Two human beings.

FREDERICKS

Okay! Measure them against the just as innocent people those two can knock off if they bluff their way out of this trap.

158

BARD

The guy's wife and kid!

FREDERICKS

Lad, you're putting a weapon in the hands of every felon in the country, you let . . .

BARD

(*Overriding*)

I didn't invent the scheme, dammit! I'm doing all I can. We've got sixty officers in those woods now . . . the streets are blocked off. . . .

FREDERICKS

Bastards like them're wily.

BARD

(*Turning to* CARSON)

Carson! Those're escapees from a Federal prison in there. You call it!

CARSON

(*Turns from window slightly*)

I'll string along with you, Deputy . . . at least until we speak to Hilliard.

FREDERICKS

O-kay, lads. It's your baby. I'm just a sour old man hates to see frisky young slobs make fools of theirselves. (*Harshly*) But pity's a luxury your badge don't afford!

(*The radio buzzes.* BARD *flips switch, picks up mike.*)

BARD

(*Into mike*)

Deputy Bard . . .

DUTCH'S VOICE

We just got another telephone report, Jess. A man's voice, unidentified, *inside* the house called a downtown hotel . . . spoke to a man named Flick . . . told him to meet a red-headed girl at Lombardi Grille . . . South Illinois Street.

BARD

(Lowers mike)

God Almighty, that's the daughter. *(Into mike)* Dutch . . . put a city detective in the Lombardi Grille. Have him pick up the man and the girl.

DUTCH'S VOICE

There's more. The one called Flick is supposed to call back to the Hilliard house . . . let the telephone ring three times, then hang up. Some sort of hanky-panky.

BARD

Thanks, Dutch. *(Flips off radio. Puts down mike)* Wonder what the devil that's all about.

CARSON

(Quietly—looking through the glasses)

Bard . . . there's some sort of activity behind the Hilliard garage. You can barely make it out in the light from the window.

BARD

(Takes glasses, looks)

Looks to me like somebody stretched out on the ground.

(Blackout)

HILLIARD HOME

> *The lights are on in the living room and in the master bedroom. The rest of the house is dim.* ELEANOR *and* RALPHIE *stand at the window of the master bed-*

room. ROBISH *is in the window in the pantry, looking out the window of the side door.* GLENN *sits on the arm of the sofa in the living room, listening to the newscaster on the radio. Though* ROBISH *begins speaking as soon as the lights are up, the radio newscaster is heard all through the beginning of the scene until* GLENN *turns the radio off.*

RADIO NEWSCASTER
(On speaker, under scene)
. . . see what the weather man has in store for us. Clear skies tomorrow, much colder, with brisk winds tomorrow and Sunday. No more rain is predicted for the Indianapolis area . . . but better dig out that overcoat because winter is almost here! This has been Kyle McGreevey, your ten-o'clock newscaster, now saying . . . good-night and good cheer!

ROBISH
(As the lights come up)
Griffin! (GLENN *does not answer, his attention on radio*) Griffin, can yuh hear me? I seen somethin' out by the garage! (*Still no answer.* ROBISH *takes an uncertain step toward the kitchen, suddenly whirls and unlocks the side door, opens it a crack, hiding behind it, gun ready, speaks in low, cautious growl*) Hey, out there? (*Turns and calls into house . . . a plea for help, lost without his "leader"*) Griffin! (*Out the door . . . slightly louder*) Listen . . . anybody out there . . . coppers . . . we'll blast the woman'n kid in here! (*Pause. The silence works on him; the uncertainty becomes turbulent*) Christ. What am I gonna . . . *Christ!* (ROBISH *closes and locks the side door, turns and goes through the kitchen door to appear in the living room.* GLENN *rises from sofa and turns off the radio. There is a growing wildness in him. Convinced now, deluding himself into thinking what he wants to believe, he enters another phase . . . in which nothing can touch him. This is in sharp contrast to the stunned glassy fear of the last*

scenes. He is gay, refusing reality, like a man with too many drinks. ROBISH, *entering the living room, cannot reach him through the following*) Griffin, yuh hear me?

GLENN

(*In soft disbelief*)

He's okay.

ROBISH

I seen . . .

GLENN

(*Mounting joy*)

Hank's okay, Robish.

ROBISH

To hell with the kid. He's in the clink. Lissen . . .
(*During the following,* CHUCK *appears at the side door outside. He lets himself in with* CINDY's *key and closes the door. He stands for a while in the pantry, listening. He moves to the pantry wall and stands with an ear against it. Then he goes up the back stairs and appears in the upstairs hall. He looks around cautiously, listens down the front stairs and then steps cautiously into* RALPHIE's *room and closes the door, leaving it slightly ajar.*)

GLENN

(*With violent relief*)

They'd have had it on the news, wouldn't they? Nothing. They're still lookin' for all of us. Not a goddam word about Hank!

ROBISH

Lissen . . . we gotta change our ideas.

162

GLENN

(*At the stairs*)

Ideas perkin' fine. Everythin's chimin'. *Hank made it!* He's on his way to Helen!

ROBISH

(*Disgusted*)

Who yuh tryin' to con? I tell yuh, I seen somethin' move out by the garage.

GLENN

(*High spirits. Laughs*)

Goblins, Robish. Like on Halloween when we was kids. God, how Hank used to go for that Halloween crap! Dress up ... burnt cork'n his face ...

ROBISH

(*Looks out window*)

Any coppers out there ...

GLENN

We're snug, we're snug. Two hours now, we'll be in Louisville. Hank's with Helen.

ROBISH

They put that on the radio, did they? Any cops stick their necks'n here, I blow up the whole goddam house.

(CHUCK *is now in* RALPHIE's *bedroom, his gun ready.*)

(*Blackout*)

THE WALLINGS' ATTIC

FREDERICKS *is still seated on the trunk.* BARD *has the glasses and is looking out the window.* CARSON *stands by.*

FREDERICKS

If there's any shooting over there . . .

BARD

(*Hands glasses to* CARSON, *turns*)
I'll give the signal to close in. Satisfied, Lieutenant?

FREDERICKS

(*Rises as* CARSON *takes up the watch through the window*)
No, I'm not. There's another gun in that house now . . .
'cause we waited.

BARD

(*Turning toward the window*)
What I'd like to know is how that kid got through the
police lines.

FREDERICKS

Plenty of ways . . . you know the neighborhood well
enough.

CARSON

(*His first show of emotion*)
A reckless muddlehead like that could botch up everything if he startles them in there!

FREDERICKS

Why shouldn't he take it in his own hands?

CARSON

If only his gun's between those two and the family somehow . . .

BARD

My hunch is the boy's layin' low . . . not knowin' where
everybody is . . . waitin' for someone to make a move . . . us
or them.

164

FREDERICKS

Lads, you're up a creek.

CARSON

The boy's smart enough to know he's done for if he doesn't get them both at the same time . . . and fast!

FREDERICKS

Lads, you're up a long, long creek and no paddles.
(*The radio buzzes.* BARD *flips switch, picks up mike.*)

BARD
(*Into mike*)

Deputy Bard . . .

WINSTON'S VOICE
(*On radio*)

Jess . . . Hilliard's on his way upstairs. Tread easy now, you guys. This gentleman's had it.
(BARD *flips off radio, puts down mike. They all wait, looking at the stairs.*)

FREDERICKS
(*As he turns*)

Man plays with dynamite, he's going to get it.
(DAN *enters up the stairs, looks around, quietly terrified but determined.*)

BARD

Evening, Mr. Hilliard. My name's Bard. Deputy Sheriff, Marion County . . . I received your letter, Mr. Hilliard.

DAN

I didn't write you any letter.

BARD

(*Taking letter out of his pocket*)
Look, Mr. Hilliard . . . we wouldn't be here if we didn't have it all pretty straight. So let's not waste . . . (*Stops, staring into* DAN's *face; then, very gently*) Sorry. You want to sit down, Mr. Hilliard?
(BARD *helps* DAN *to box where he sits beside the radio equipment, back to audience.*)

DAN
(*Flatly*)
Where'd I slip up?

BARD

You didn't. Young Griffin's dead. He had your gun.

DAN
(*The name sinking in . . . recognition*)
Bard . . . Bard . . . do you know a man named Flick?

BARD

I've heard the name.

DAN

My daughter's paying Flick two thousand dollars to kill you.

BARD

So . . . (*In wonder*) So that's the way he was going to do it. (*Briskly*) Well, Mr. Flick's being arrested, right about now . . . Lombardi Grille . . .

DAN
(*Rises, steps threateningly toward* BARD)
You fool! You damned clumsy . . .

166

BARD

Okay, Hilliard. Let off steam. Take a swing. How'd I know what they'd send your girl into? I swear . . .

DAN

Swear? What can you swear to? That when I'm not back in there in time . . . when Flick doesn't call . . . they won't jump to the conclusion that . . . (*Breaks off*) What can anyone swear to?

BARD

Don't worry about Flick's call, Mr. Hilliard. We know the signal. We can handle it.

DAN
(*Picks up rifle with telescopic sight*)
Are you planning to use this?

FREDERICKS

They both still in there?

DAN

Yes.

BARD
(*Takes rifle from* DAN, *replaces it*)
How many guns?

DAN
(*Looks out window toward his own house*)
One. With three bullets.

FREDERICKS

That helps!

DAN
(*Turns from window. Slowly*)
Also . . . my wife and son.

FREDERICKS

Mr. Hilliard—if these two convicts get away with this scheme . . .

DAN

I don't care about that now. I don't want them . . . or you . . . to kill my wife or boy. That's first. *First.* God help me, that comes first.

BARD

Nobody' blaming you, Mr. Hilliard. Nobody in his right mind can raise a voice against what you've done . . . But I can't let you go back in there.
> (*Pause. Then, slowly,* DAN *takes the special delivery envelope containing money from his inside topcoat pocket. He hands it to* BARD, *who examines the contents.*)

DAN

Until they get that . . . they're not coming out.

FREDERICKS
(*Crisply*)

Then we move in.

DAN
(*Erupting*)

What'm I supposed to do . . . *sit up here and watch it happen?*

FREDERICKS

It's plain suicide for you to go back in there now!

DAN
(*A look at the window*)

That may be. There comes a time when that fact just doesn't enter in . . . You don't give a hang about a life or two . . . what's one more?

168

BARD

(Drops envelope with money on box; he is having an inner struggle)

Mr. Hilliard . . . we're trying to help you.

DAN

(Pleading forcefully, hopelessly)

Then clear out! Get away. Take your men . . . your rifles . . . your floodlights . . . and *get away!*

    (CARSON steps in, picks up the envelope with the money and holds it out to DAN.)

CARSON

We can't do that, Mr. Hilliard. I'll give you ten minutes . . . from the time you walk through that door over there. Shortly after you're inside, we'll give them the telephone signal they're waiting for. If you need us, flicker a light. You've got ten minutes. It's on your shoulders.

    (Pause. DAN takes the envelope. CARSON steps back.)

BARD

Mr. Hilliard, you'd better have the whole picture. Charles Wright is in the house.

DAN

(Amazed. Turns to BARD)

Chuck?

BARD

And he's armed. We couldn't prevent it. *(Slight pause)* Do you want a gun, Mr. Hilliard?

DAN

(Quietly)

No . . . thanks.

    (He puts the envelope into his inside topcoat pocket.)

169

BARD

They search you when you come in? (DAN *nods slowly*)
Good luck . . . sir.

    (DAN *turns to the stairs . . . then stops . . . turns.*)

DAN

I've changed my mind.

BARD

You want a gun?

DAN

Please.

    (BARD *takes his own revolver from his holster and
hands it to* DAN.)

BARD

You know how to use it?

    (DAN *looks at revolver, nods, breaks it and shakes the
bullets into his hand, examines the empty chamber.*)

FREDERICKS

(*Shocked*)

Are you crazy?

DAN

Maybe. Only a crazy man'd go in there with an empty gun.
Griffin doesn't think I'm crazy.

BARD

That's a pretty long shot, isn't it?

DAN

I don't have any short ones in sight. Do you?

    (DAN *firmly puts the bullets into* BARD's *hand. Then,
he turns and goes down the stairs. Pause. Then* BARD
flips the switch on the radio, picks up mike.)

BARD
(Into mike)

Car nine . . . Winston.

WINSTON'S VOICE

Parked in side drive, Jess.

BARD

Tom . . . take Mr. Hilliard back to his car. (BARD *puts down the mike, flips off the radio; thoughtfully*) How'd you like to be riding up to *your* door like that, Fredericks?

FREDERICKS

Just luck I'm not. Or you.

BARD

Yeah. They didn't happen to pick on us, that's all.
(BARD *picks up binoculars from window sill.* CARSON *looks at his watch.*)

(Blackout)

HILLIARD HOME

The lights are on in the living room; the rest of the house is dim. ELEANOR *and* RALPHIE *are in the master bedroom at the window.* CHUCK *still stands in* RALPHIE'S *room with the door open, listening, waiting.* GLENN *is at the window in the living room.* ROBISH *is turning from the window in the side door in the pantry.*

ROBISH

(Calling as he moves toward living room)
Here he comes, Griffin!

171

GLENN

(*Exhilarated*)

Only two hours now, Robish. Two lousy hours! I'll do the drivin', make it in less!

ROBISH

(*As he enters the living room*)

The little gal ain't with him.

(*Above, CHUCK steps into the upstairs hall, listening.*)

GLENN

Who cares? Who gives a damn?

(*GLENN steps to the door, unlocks and opens it. DAN stands in the doorway, his hands in his topcoat pockets. DAN comes into the room. GLENN closes and locks the door and moves to DAN. GLENN's mood is almost a travesty on his previous behavior. DAN's manner is profoundly quiet, as he sizes up the situation, frowning at the strange change in GLENN.*)

ROBISH

(*At foot of stairs*)

Hand over the dough, Hilliard.

DAN

(*Ignores this, lifts voice*)

Stay up there, Ellie. Keep the door locked.

ROBISH

Yuh hear me?

DAN

(*Flatly—almost a challenge*)

I don't have it.

172

ROBISH
(*Roaring*)

What?

GLENN

Now, Pop . . . who you kiddin'? Take your hands outta
your pockets . . . *please.*
(*This is what* DAN *wants. He does so, facing* GLENN.
GLENN *frisks him, feels the gun in the pocket, reaches
in.*)

ROBISH

I'll take the cash, Griffin.
(GLENN *takes the gun out of* DAN's *pocket with his
right hand, looking into* DAN's *eyes.*)

GLENN

What'd you say, Robish? (*He whips the gun out, points it
at* ROBISH *and pushes* DAN *around behind him*) I didn't hear
you, Robish!
(ROBISH *stares at the gun, lowering his own.*)

ROBISH
(*Steps toward* DAN)

You lousy sonofa . . .

GLENN
(*Laughs*)

Had it all doped, didn't you? (*He reaches with his left hand
across his own body, keeping the aim on* ROBISH, *into* DAN's
inside coat pocket . . . brings out the envelope) This what you
had in mind, Robish?

ROBISH
(*To* DAN)

You bastard!

173

GLENN

(*Stepping toward* ROBISH, *who backs away*)
Not Pop. Not my old pal Pops! (*Pockets the money*) Any
objections, Robish?

ROBISH

Let's get outta here.
(*The telephone rings.* ROBISH *makes a move to answer
it.*)

GLENN

Stay away from it, Robish. (*They all stand and listen in
frozen silence while the phone rings three times: spaced,
automatic.* GLENN *waits after the third ring until he's sure
that there won't be a fourth. He laughs*) Well, that takes care
of Bard! Time to break up housekeeping.
(*Above,* ELEANOR *moves to bedroom door, switches
on the bedroom lights and opens the door. She sees
*CHUCK *in the hall, gasps. He turns to her and signals
her to silence. She closes and locks the door and stands
with* RALPHIE, *who has come to her side.*)

ROBISH

(*As action takes place above*)
Let's get movin'.

DAN

Griffin . . . you'd better take me along. *Only* me!

ROBISH

Like hell. We gotta have a dame in the car.
(GLENN *has stopped on the stair, looks at* DAN.)

DAN

Griffin . . . I'm the only one who knows you hired a man
named Flick to kill Bard.

GLENN
(*Makes the "clickety-click" gesture*)
Right up to the very end!

DAN
You'd better take me along.

GLENN
Nothin' can touch me now, Hilliard! Everythin's goin' my way!

ROBISH
Come on. Them woods out there could be full-a Feds, all we know.

GLENN
And you . . . you, Hilliard, can come along, too. 'Cause it's like this, see—Hank's waitin'.

DAN
Waiting?

ROBISH
You're off your rocker!

GLENN
So I'm in a kinda hurry! (*He goes to the stairs and up.* CHUCK *steps into* RALPHIE's *room and closes the door*) Hey, missus, get the brat ready. We're goin' on a little picnic.
(*He reaches the door of the bedroom.* ELEANOR *and* RALPHIE *move away from the door.*)

ROBISH
(*Covers* DAN *with pistol*)
He's gettin' some sense back.
(GLENN *tries the bedroom door.*)

GLENN

Hey, folks, you don' wanna miss the fun. The ice cream'll be all et up! (*He knocks on the door*) Lady, you don' want me to have to kick in this nice shiny door, do you?

(GLENN *steps back, lifts his leg and kicks the door; it splinters. At the same moment,* CHUCK *opens the door of* RALPHIE'S *bedroom and steps behind* GLENN, *lifting his gun. He brings it down with great force on* GLENN'S *head behind the ear;* GLENN *spins and falls backward into* RALPHIE'S *bedroom.* CHUCK *plunges down the stairs.*)

ROBISH

No racket up there! No noise!

(DAN *sees* CHUCK *descending the stairs, gun in hand;* DAN *ducks into dining-room door, as* ROBISH *catches sight of* CHUCK. ROBISH *fires, hitting* CHUCK, *whose gun explodes toward the floor.* CHUCK, *clutching his shoulder, falls across living-room floor.* ROBISH, *out of control, unthinking now, throws open the front door. Above,* ELEANOR—*hearing the shots*—*runs out of the bedroom and comes down the stairs wildly, leaving* RALPHIE *alone in the bedroom. Outside, floodlights illuminate the whole house in a harsh cold light.*)

ELEANOR

Dan? . . .

DAN
(*Shouting*)

Stay there, Ellie!

ROBISH
(*In open door, shouting*)

Hey, out there! You hear me out there, coppers? (*As* DAN *moves cautiously toward* ROBISH'S *back*) I got one of yuh! Who wants it next?

(DAN *moves fast now, driving his shoulder into* RO-
BISH's *back, sending him catapulting out the front
door.* DAN *slams, locks door, as* ELEANOR *comes plung-
ing down the stairs, heedless.*)

ELEANOR

Dan, Dan . . .
(DAN *grabs* ELEANOR, *swings her across the room, out
of line of the front door. Above,* RALPHIE *starts out of
master bedroom just as* GLENN *lifts himself to his feet
in* RALPHIE's *bedroom, regaining consciousness.* GLENN
and RALPHIE *meet at door of master bedroom.* GLENN,
rubbing his head, turns the gun on RALPHIE *and backs
him into the bedroom as:*)

(*Blackout*)

THE WALLINGS' ATTIC
CARSON *is kneeling in the window with the binoculars, looking out.* BARD *stands behind him with the
rifle pointed out, looking through the telescopic sight.*

BARD

It's Robish . . .

CARSON

Get him, Jesse. I'll give the signal to close in.

BARD
(*Lowering the rifle*)
Somebody pushed him out that door.

CARSON

He's heading for the car. Get him, Jesse!

BARD

Five minutes, Carson. Give Hilliard five more minutes!

CARSON

Hilliard might be dead!

BARD

Harry, I'm pleading with you. *Somebody shoved that big guy out the door. Five minutes!*
>*(Slight pause.* CARSON *turns, still kneeling, switches on radio, picks up mike.)*

CARSON

All right, Jess. (*Into mike*) Fredericks . . . Robish is in the Hilliard car. He's armed. Stop him.
>(BARD *picks up the PA mike and speaks into it.)*

BARD

>(*His voice sounding in distance over PA*)

Hilliard. Do you need us? *Hilliard.*

(*Blackout*)

HILLIARD HOME
>*Outside, the floodlights remain on. There is light in living room and in master bedroom.* GLENN, *still groggy from the blow, is in bedroom, gun on* RALPHIE, *who is against the wall. In the living room,* DAN *and* ELEANOR *are helping* CHUCK *toward front door; he cannot stand without support.*

BARD'S VOICE
>(*The hollow sound of PA system*)

Hilliard, can you hear me?

DAN

Get him out of here!
(DAN *unlocks and opens front door*)

CHUCK

I flubbed it, didn't I?

DAN

(*Stepping out, waves off*)
Hold fire out there!

RALPHIE

(*In bedroom above—as* GLENN *grabs him and holds him in front of himself as a shield*)
Dad! Dad!

DAN

(*As he and* ELEANOR *get* CHUCK *to door*)
Get this boy some help.

CHUCK

(*Faintly*)
I . . . I couldn't do anything else, I . . .

DAN

(*Taking the pistol from his hand*)
You won't need this, son.

ELEANOR

(*Urgently, as she goes out with* CHUCK)
Ralphie!

DAN

(*Firmly*)
Ralphie's all right!
(ELEANOR *and* CHUCK *go out door.* DAN *turns, looking at pistol he has taken from* CHUCK. *He leaves the front door open wide.*)

179

GLENN
(Calling)
I'm with him, Hilliard.

RALPHIE

Dad . . . are you coming?

DAN

(Puts pistol in his pocket, turns to stairs; speaks with grim determination)
I'm coming, son!

GLENN

In here, Hilliard. *(As* DAN *enters bedroom)* I'm still gonna make it . . . still gonna pull it off. *(As* DAN *stops)* You're gonna get me outta this.

DAN

(Firmly, tonelessly)
Let go of the boy, Griffin.

GLENN

Fat chance, them coppers out there!

BARD'S VOICE
(Over PA)
Griffin . . . Come out with your hands up . . . No gun!
*(*DAN *steps to window, opens it, calls out.)*

DAN

Stay out of here. Turn off the light! *(The floodlights go out.* DAN *turns to* GLENN*)* Now. Take your hands off him.
*(*GLENN *does so, but places the gun at back of* RALPHIE'S *neck)*

GLENN

You move, kid, I'll blow your head off.

DAN

(*Gently, urgently*)

Ralph . . . listen to me. That man is not going to hurt you.

GLENN

Try budgin', kid, you'll find out.

DAN

He's not going to hurt you at all because . . .

GLENN

Lay off, my head's bustin', Hank's waitin', lay off . . .

DAN

Ralph . . . have I ever lied to you?
(RALPHIE *shakes his head.*)

GLENN

(*Gun against* RALPHIE's *neck*)

Feel that? . . .

DAN

(*To* RALPHIE)

Now—I want you to do exactly as I tell you. Because that gun is not loaded.

GLENN

Stop bluffin', Hilliard, and let's get . . .

DAN

It has no bullets in it, Ralph. Do you understand that?
(RALPHIE *nods.*)

GLENN

You're lyin'! You wouldn't've brung it in here if . . .

DAN

(Stepping slightly, to clear the way; shouts)
Run!
(Without hesitation, RALPHIE obeys. He runs . . . fast. He goes out of the bedroom, down the stairs and out the front door. As he starts, GLENN pulls the trigger of the revolver. There is a click. GLENN is astonished. Then, he tries again and again. A dazed bleak horror mounts GLENN's face. He starts for DAN, raising the gun to strike him. The sound of an ambulance siren is heard starting up and fading in the distance. DAN brings out CHUCK's pistol and holds it pointed at GLENN.)

GLENN

(As he starts to strike DAN)
You goddam . . .
(He breaks off, staring at the pistol in DAN's hand, incredulous. Long pause.)

DAN

Why don't you say something, Griffin? Clickety-clickety-click. *(Steps closer)* You're not talking. Where's your voice now? *Call me Pop. Say* something, *damn you!*

GLENN

It ain't gonna be like this . . . Hank's waitin' . . .

DAN

(Almost brutally)
Griffin . . . your brother's not waiting anywhere. He's dead!
(GLENN is glassy-eyed, stunned) Full of police bullets. *Dead!*

182

GLENN
(*Suddenly wild*)
You're lyin', I don't believe . . . you're lyin'!!

DAN
You did that, too, damn you. . . . *Damn you!*
(*The life goes out of* GLENN. *He swings full circle now
. . . back to the stunned, depressed, lifeless phase of
earlier in the evening. Despair . . . and worse. From
now on he has no desire to survive. What follows is
the death-wish all the way . . . finally erupting in his
attempt to goad* DAN *into killing.*)

DAN
It's your turn, Griffin . . . how do you like it?

GLENN
(*Bleakly*)
Go ahead . . . (*Lifelessly*) Get it over with. . . .

DAN
You don't like waiting? I've waited for hours . . . all of
us . . like years . . . all night . . . two days . . .

GLENN
Get it over with! (*He senses the hesitation in* DAN, *changes
his tactics shrewdly*) You ain't got it in you!

DAN
(*Low, hard*)
I've got it in me. *You* put it there!

GLENN
(*Goading*)
Then go ahead!

BARD'S VOICE

(*On the PA*)

Hilliard, can you hear me? . . . Your wife's here. And the boy. They're both safe!

(*Pause.* GLENN *and* DAN *are both staring.*)

GLENN

You ain't got it in you!

(DAN *tenses with the revolver pointed at* GLENN. *Then, suddenly realizing what he has almost done, he lowers the gun, relieved.*)

DAN

(*Quietly*)

You're right. (*Low—with disgust*) Thank God, you're right! (*Quietly—with great dignity*) Get out of my house. (*Then he steps to* GLENN *and slaps him a resounding, violent blow across the face*) Get out of my house!

(GLENN *is staggered by the blow. He recoils. There is a pause while* GLENN *cowers, rubbing his jaw. Then,* GLENN *begins muttering, dazed.*)

GLENN

(*His voice whining . . . self-pity . . . a boy again*)

I'm gettin' out, Pop . . . I'm goin'. Only I'm takin' Hank along. You hit me for the last goddam time. . . . You ain't ever gonna hit Hank or me again. (*He moves toward the bedroom door as* DAN *steps out of his way*) I'm takin' Hank along and you ain't gonna see either one of us ever again! (*He turns in the upstairs hall and shouts back at* DAN *in the bedroom*) You can sit here'n rot in your stinkin' house, Mister God! I hated this crummy joint the day I was born!

(GLENN *turns and starts down the stairs as* DAN *follows him to the bedroom door.*)

DAN

(*In amazement; weary disgust*)

Get out.

GLENN

(*On his way downstairs*)

You ain't gonna beat it into Hank'n me! Hank'n me's gonna be right on top! (GLENN, *now at the foot of the stairs, pauses, looks around, still dazed.* DAN *follows him down the stairs, pauses on lower step.* GLENN *turns toward the open door, beckoning to an imaginary* HANK) C'mon, Hank . . . we'll show 'em! (*The floodlights come on outside as* GLENN *steps in the doorway brandishing the gun. He goes out of sight, shouting*) We'll show 'em, Hank, we'll show 'em, Hank, we'll . . .

(*A rifle shot is heard, echoing down the quiet street.* DAN *stands quietly on the stairs. . . . Lights remain on in Hilliard home.*)

THE WALLINGS' ATTIC

Lights rise on the attic. BARD *is lowering the rifle. He looks at* CARSON *a moment, a strange expression on his face.*

CARSON

(*Almost reassuringly*)

He asked for it, Jess. He . . . he acted like he was begging for it.

(BARD *looks at the rifle, then places it against the wall; slowly sits on the box.*)

CARSON

You going over there?

BARD

(*Softly*)

In a little while.

CARSON

You feel all right, Jess?

BARD

Just . . . maybe a little disgusted with the human race.

CARSON

Mmmm. Including Hilliard?

BARD

(*Looks up at him, smiles wanly*)
Thanks, Harry. . . . No, *not* including Hilliard.

CARSON

World's full of Hilliards.
(CARSON *turns and goes down the attic stairs.* BARD *sits quietly, thinking . . . as the lights fade slowly on the attic scene.*

In the Hilliard home, DAN *still stands unmoving on the stairs.* ELEANOR *appears at front door; she looks stunned, worn. She gazes at the havoc that was her home. She moves slowly to the sofa, almost helplessly rearranges a pillow.* RALPHIE *enters behind her; he crosses to* DAN, *whose head is down;* RALPHIE *stands gazing at his father. . . . Outside,* CINDY *appears and enters the pantry, disappears into kitchen a moment. As* CINDY *enters the living room from dining room,* DAN *lifts his head, looks at her; then, slowly, he turns his gaze on* ELEANOR. *Their eyes meet, hold. They stand looking at each other as though cognizant of the miracle . . . as though seeing in each other, and perhaps in the world, more than words could convey.*)

(*Dimout*)

Slow curtain